Glass in Canada

The First One Hundred Years

Glass in Canada

GERALD STEVENS

Foreword by Ralph Hedlin and Heidi Redekop

METHUEN

Toronto   New York   London   Sydney   Auckland

CANADIAN CATALOGUING IN PUBLICATION DATA

Stevens, Gerald ca. 1912-1981

Glass in Canada

ISBN 0-458-95430-6

1. Glass—Canada—History. I. Title

EDITORS: Ralph Hedlin and Heidi Redekop
PROJECT MANAGER: James T. Wills
PHOTOGRAPHY: Blake McKendry
DESIGN: Brant Cowie/Artplus Ltd.
TYPESETTING: Compeer Typographic Services Limited
FILM: Graphic Litho-Plate Ltd.
PRINTING: Ashton-Potter Limited
BINDING: The Hunter Rose Company

Printed and Bound in Canada

1234 82 83 84 85

Contents

FOREWORD

GERALD AND EDITH (BEA) STEVENS did not live to see the completion of Gerald's last book upon which both, with us, had worked so hard.

Gerald Stevens made an unparalleled contribution—greatly aided by Bea—to the understanding, documentation and appreciation of the heritage of this nation in all its forms—glass, furniture, guns, paintings, silver, woodenwares—the whole range of the work of our artists and artisans. The books by Gerald Stevens, the first of which appeared twenty-seven years ago, remain a primary source for researcher and collector.

Gerald's great artistic commitment and sensitivity was not paralleled by an equivalent commercial skill. Gerald and Bea experienced hard times for all the years we knew them. In their mature years they lived in Toronto with Bea's niece and her husband, the generous Audrey and Lloyd Bruce. In later years, the Stevens spent their winters in our home, and we shared their lives.

They had a unique and important collection of authenticated Canadian glass in storage. Gerald would not entertain the thought of being separated from it. He really couldn't afford to keep it.

He propounded a possible solution at dinner at our home one night: if we would buy the collection he would receive money he badly needed and would still be able to live with the glass much of the time, and he could use specimens for the public lectures he still gave and for the teaching of both of us. Further, it would be possible then to prepare detailed records for a book, useful to Canadian collectors and important as a record of authenticated glass. Only pieces that he could authenticate, from his own encyclopedic knowledge of Canadian glass, would be included. Most importantly, there would be a permanent record of known Canadian artists in glass and of the whimseys they had made and that Gerald and Bea had studied and collected for so long.

We were, frankly, a little startled. We rather agreed with Bea, who mischievously suggested: "Gerald, if you talk Heidi and Ralph into this you'll prove for a fact that it is possible to have your cake and eat it too!" But Gerald's enthusiasm was not to be denied. We sought moneyed corporate sponsors, but with no success. We finally agreed to Gerald's proposition, subject to the condition that he would undertake to write all he knew of every piece. If a book finally did result, we would try to arrange publication. And so started the long process of studying, annotating, authenticating and interviewing.

Finally, the recording of information on every piece was almost complete. We spent a four-day March weekend in 1978 working on final sections in the small apartment in Barrie where Gerald and Bea were wintering.

A few days later Audrey Bruce phoned to tell us that Bea had been taken suddenly ill. Before we reached Barrie, Bea was dead.

Gerald and Bea had lived so long, so fruitfully and so happily together that they effectively died together: by the next day all of Gerald's recollection of the past had been wiped away as if by a sponge. He had no memory of Bea alive and no awareness that Bea was dead. Some time later he, too, passed to the haven of the hereafter, already inevitably enlivened by Bea Stevens' warm laughter and her puckish sense of fun.

We had no heart for the sorting, organization, photographing and editing that remained to be done. For two years the material of this book lay untouched in our files. But our promise had been given. The story of Gerald's and Bea's long years in the pursuit of Canadian glass and Canadian glassblowers must be told.

This is that story, words and pictures. It is their story, not ours, but we are honoured to be a part of its telling. And it is our warm hope that, as Gerald so fervently wished, through it will be added something useful, not only to the descriptive literature and the understanding of glass made by early Canadian artisans but, more particularly, of the artists in glass who made it.

RALPH HEDLIN AND HEIDI REDEKOP
Toronto

EDITORS' ACKNOWLEDGEMENTS

THIS BOOK is *by* Gerald Stevens in the literal sense of the word. However, Bea's death and Gerald's incapacity and subsequent death meant that, unhappily in their absence, a number of loose ends had to be drawn together, unpolished manuscripts prepared for publication, pictures taken and a book constructed.

Many people became involved, under our overall editorship. Among them they photographed the collection, ensured that Gerald's captions were with the right pieces, typed and proofed manuscript and performed a seeming infinity of tasks that demanded close attention.

The commitments of time, knowledge, skill and dedication of Bea Stevens eclipsed that of everyone else, save only the author, Gerald Stevens. Mrs. Stevens' niece, Audrey Bruce, and her husband, Lloyd, provided essential support and help. David Tyrer, a Toronto collector, took an early interest and brought us in contact with Jim Wills and Blake McKendry who, respectively, provided editorial direction and photographed the entire collection and, beyond this, provided enthusiastic support. In the absence of Jim Wills' personal commitment the production of this book would not have been accomplished.

The list of dealers and collectors who took an interest in the effort of the Stevens and the Hedlins to find important new pieces is far too long to include in its entirety. However, it would be a serious remission to fail to formally acknowledge the contributions of such Ontario dealers as Margaret and Mogens Philip, until recently owner-operators of Canadian Homestead Antiques at Markham; of the late Lena Stanbury of Unionville; of Bill Cole, still very active at Oro Station; of Sally Earle, long an important glass dealer at Napanee; and, more recently, of Joyce Byrne of Montreal; as well as Fay Stettler of the Curiosity Shop in Winnipeg.

Ramona Antaya of Toronto was invaluable in the management and control of the manuscript, as well as the word processing. Susan Schindle of Winnipeg, Miss Redekop's sister, was equally invaluable in the collating of the material.

Most major projects involve many people. This was no different. Gerald and Bea Stevens and their editors are indebted to those named and others unnamed—an indebtedness that is here gratefully acknowledged.

RALPH HEDLIN AND HEIDI REDEKOP

PREFACE

MY PREVIOUS BOOKS and writing on Canadian glass have been directed toward the researcher, to the broadening of the appreciation of the accomplishments of early Canadian glassworkers and the history and production of our early glass factories. In the many, many years of work and research I have proven many patterns, whimseys and individual pieces of glass as being Canadian. Working closely with my wife, Bea Stevens, and with my friends and students, Ralph Hedlin and his wife, Heidi Redekop, I have selected Canadian pieces and prepared notes on each. This book is the result. It is, in some small way, a part payment of a debt that I have to the many researchers, librarians, archivists, museums, glassworkers, collectors and others who have encouraged or assisted me in a lifetime of work in the Canadian decorative arts, including early Canadian glass.

My background perhaps provides me with a somewhat unique opportunity to evaluate the tremendous upsurge of interest in the cultural past of our nation as presented by these decorative arts.

As a youth, my father, the late Frank Stevens, spent his summer holidays as an apprentice cabinet-maker in the furniture shop of my paternal grandfather in Leeds County, Ontario. Later still he moved to Montreal and became associated with the firm of W. Scott and Sons, leading 19th century dealers in paintings, rugs and objects d'art.

My first coherent thought included dim visions of oils, water-colours, prints and other media associated with paintings, cabinet- and rug-making. As a young boy, my greatest delight on a Saturday afternoon was to climb the seat of a quite splendid van drawn by a gigantic glossy black horse and help the French-Canadian driver deliver old Dutch Masters to the financial elite of Montreal.

Those were the days when Canadian art was reserved for the fourth floor hall or the scullery maid's bedroom.

Later memories include: watching Marc-Aurèle de Foy Suzor-Côté deliver an unwrapped pastel painting to 99 Notre Dame Street West, absentmindedly place it on a chair, then seat himself on the same chair; ascending to an upper floor in the same building to visit the Canadian studio of James Wilson Morrice; watching Maurice Cullen carving frames to fit his own work; and, later, dropping in on F. S. Coburn and helping carry out one of his larger canvases to the waiting van.

My first lengthy drive in an automobile was to visit the Island of Orleans studio of Horatio Walker, where I listened to my father and Walker discuss a forthcoming one-man show.

Later still, I was honoured by private lessons on evaluation of pigments, restoration and so forth from Richard Jack, R.A., R.C.A., and Frederic Simpson Coburn, R.C.A. A failed painter, I nevertheless absorbed knowledge relative to art and the financial problems confronting contemporary artists. This knowledge was to contribute to a sympathetic understanding when, as an art dealer, I bought and sold paintings.

This rather sketchy biography leads up to the first important gallery exhibition I staged, a one-man show of thirty-one paintings by Cornelius Kreighoff. The exhibition opened on May 12, 1945. The largest canvas, a portage scene, sold for $2,200. It was the largest known example of an autumn painting by this artist.

The gallery sold sketches by Tom Thomson, ranging from $50 to $100; A. Y. Jackson, a picked example for $35; J. W. Morrice, small wooden panel, $50; Clarence Gagnon, Canadian winter scenes, $35 – $50. Such prices required a hard sell. Clients took hours of convincing that they should invest their money in Canadian art.

The same applied to early Canadian furniture, silver, books and especially glass. Indeed, every category of Canadiana went begging for a home. This was a period when few Canadian museums gave recognition to Canadiana, other than archaeological artifacts and paintings. Little research had been undertaken and proof of early Canadian skills was lacking. Other than a dedicated few, collectors assumed anything having quality in design or craftsmanship must have been imported from France, England or the United States. The very thought that Canadian craftsmen could have produced anything other than pine furniture and a few second rate items in hardwood was seldom given serious consideration. And as for Upper Canada, early craftsmen had spent their time in building log cabins and filling these hovels with crudely made benches and trundle beds!

Examples of the values of the period included the Ste. Genevieve commodes, offered for $50 – $250, and firearms, made in Canada, at $25 – $35. Canadiana silver items then offered at $200 – $250 presently are many times that price. The list is endless. Only those institutions gifted with vision and confidence, as well as knowledge of our historic past, profited from such a fantastic and degrading period in Canadian awareness.

As this was the evaluation of native Canadians, can we blame the critics and historians of other countries for failing to give credit where credit was due and publicly attributing many pieces of Canadiana to craftsmen of other nationalities? Major works published less than thirty-five years ago in England and on the Continent classified silver, glass, furniture and treen produced in many countries, including the United States; if there was mention of something attributed to Canada, the object was credited elsewhere or a somewhat scathing remark was included.

This was the period when Canadians allowed, indeed insisted, that American dealers from New York, Boston and elsewhere rush north of the border accompanied by large trucks and loaded cheque books to scour the border areas of Quebec and Ontario for all manner of artifacts of merit. It is we who were guilty, not they. We should not blame them for their foresight. They had researched and published on their early artifacts, crafts and craftsmen. It was obvious to them that American skill and know-how had travelled north and northeast with the Loyalists. We were inept and appeared to cherish our ineptitude. Our authors were neglected, and their works sold at remainder counters.

Splendid examples of this were the reference books, *Canadian Landscape Painters*, by Albert H. Robson, published by The Ryerson Press, Toronto, 1932, and Marius Barbeau's *Cornelius Kreighoff* of 1934. Both of these works, offered for $5, were not bought by collectors or the public and remaindered at less than $1 a volume. I know this as a fact, because I acquired dozens of each title and gave them away when I sold a painting that was listed or documented in either work.

We have much to atone for. Present conditions, however, are fantastically different. Museums, collectors and corporations, and there are dozens more each day, vie with each other to acquire examples of authentic Canadiana: furniture, china, pottery, paintings, glass, tole, treen, and so forth are currently offered and acquired at astonishingly high prices.

Everywhere are evidences of short supply and higher costs. The good old days are finished. Country-type pickers and dealers complain of scarcity and demand prices comparable to those asked on Sherbrooke in Montreal and Bloor Street in Toronto. The Eastern Townships of Quebec, long a seemingly bottomless supply chest, have little to offer the discriminating buyer.

I must, of course, qualify this statement. You can find good items, but they are in short supply compared to years ago. There is an amazing lack of even what might be termed trivia, as represented by early maple sugar moulds, wrought iron, tole and treen. Indeed, authentic examples are very scarce and when found are quite expensive. Competition, public and private, continues to deplete the supply and increase the price.

The demand for Canadiana by a more knowledgeable public continues to grow. Faster vehicles and improved means of transportation and communication have provided the dealer and the public with the ability to travel longer distances to acquire stock in trade. I find items from Nova Scotia offered in Ontario and Quebec, Quebec furniture offered in Ontario and, unbelieveably, furniture, burl bowls and so forth from Ontario offered in Quebec. What an interchange! Our early artifacts are being worn out through excessive travel on trucks! Competition is extremely keen, and the great finds of the past are increasingly rare.

For the newer collector, Canadian glass still provides a special opportunity. Although prices have greatly increased, the individual pieces, especially of pressed Canadian glass, are still affordable. The persistent collector can put together a good collection, secure in the knowledge of contributing to the preservation of Canadian heritage. A good collection of Canadian lamps or goblets or tableware, which would have involved the commitment of a few hundred dollars, at most, some years ago, might cost a few thousand dollars today. However, given the enthusiasm of collectors and the fact that the supply is constantly reduced through breakage, an equivalent collection is likely to involve a very much larger sum ten years in the future.

The most important pieces for the collector of Canadian glass are the whimseys known to have been made by a named Canadian artist who worked in glass. A large part of the emphasis of this book is on these whimseys—non-commercial items not made for sale—including paperweights, doorstops, drapes, hats, hammers, axes, batons, rolling pins, bells, gavels, walking sticks, witch balls, animal and bird forms and others. All the whimseys illustrated in this volume were made in Canada. Collectors should study any similar whimsey they might find against these illustrations, and, if it appears similar, spend time on researching the history of the individual piece to try and establish its origins, its maker and its authenticity.

Whimseys are rare and special items that illustrate the special skills of the glassblower. They are of the utmost importance in the history of Canadian glass. A good paperweight or hat or other whimsey that is authenticated as Canadian is as important a find to the serious collector of glass as is the discovery of a previously unknown Krieghoff or Tom Thomson to the serious student of Canadian art.

A piece of Mallorytown glass, of course, would be the prized piece in any collection of Canadian glass. The author knows of only four fully authenticated pieces in private hands. Three of them are illustrated in this book. It is possible that fortunate collectors could discover additional pieces and authenticate them. Authenticated examples can be studied in the Edith Chown Pierce—Gerald Stevens Collection at the Sigmund Samuel Canadiana Gallery, Royal Ontario Museum.

Pressed glass is more easily found, even today, and is more readily identifiable than Canadian whimseys. More than thirty years of research and collecting Canadian glass has resulted in the authentication of the pieces and patterns that are included in this book. This body of knowledge has been laboriously built during long years of study, involving excavation, study of shards, interviews with glass-blowers who worked in the factories, interviews with descendants of glassblowers, research in old catalogues, newspapers and other records of the period and the exchange of information with such researchers and collectors as Edith Chown Pierce, Lorne Pierce, F. St. George Spendlove and others.

The pieces published here, many of them for the first time, were made in Canada by Canadian artisans. The collector must be aware, however, that glass workers moved across international boundaries and frequently exchanged moulds or had their own moulds. As a consequence, many fully authenticated Canadian patterns were also made in the United States. Some U.S. glass factories imprinted a trade mark, some did not. But this interchangeability does not justify, in my strongly held opinion, the recent tendency to lump pressed glass that was made in Canada as "North American." This view risks the loss of an important facet of our artistic heritage, denies our artists and artisans the recognition, acknowledgement and credit that is their due. Canadian pressed glass is an important part of Canadian heritage. Why should we abandon it to the Americans? Much of it is uniquely Canadian, and all is a worthy subject for the attention of the serious collector.

Early Canadian cut glass should receive much more attention. Much of it is signed and, even if not signed, the patterns are identifiable from old catalogues. It is an important category of Canadian glass that is largely neglected by researchers and collectors.

The encouragement of our collectors is one of the reasons for the publication of this book. Old and new Canadian collectors alike must be informed and even excited by the accomplishment of our early artists and artisans who worked in glass. Indiscriminate and undocumented collecting and exhibiting alone is not enough to ensure their recognition. Books, exhibitions and collections of each early skill are of the utmost importance. We must give particular attention to objects that can be classified as being peculiar or unique to Canada, or simply made or cut in early Canada. In this manner we can establish that which is identifiable as Canadian, rather than merely North American. The important challenge is greater selectivity and increased knowledge of our early Canadian artifacts.

An object in itself supplies visual evidence which could provide better understanding of our heritage. The object provides contact with all the senses, while thoughts and concepts are ethereal. One significant and authenticated object is worth a thousand words in the recognition and acknowledgement of our early artists and artisans and the appreciation of our national heritage.

To loosely define glass as "North American" is not to authenticate it at all. The need is for a new generation of researchers and collectors, committed to deepening the knowledge of Canadian glass, broadening the appreciation of this art form and faithfully continuing the work on Canadian glass and glassblowers that has already been well begun. In the absence of such a commitment there is a risk that the identity of this glass will be lost to future generations of Canadians.

If this book contributes to the inspiration of new research and the stimulation of serious collecting and study of our dwindling supplies of Canadian glass, it will have accomplished its purpose.

GERALD STEVENS

MALLORYTOWN

I
T IS HIGHLY PROBABLE that the first batch of glass produced in Canada was mixed at the Mallorytown Glass Works, one mile west of Mallorytown in eastern Ontario. Mallorytown is the earliest fully proven glass works in Canada. It operated in the second quarter of the last century, existed only in the folklore of the district for the first half of this century and was finally rediscovered and proven on August 18, 1953, by myself and Edith (Bea) Stevens.

The story of the long search and final success has been told many times and will not be repeated here. Perhaps the fullest account is in *Early Canadian Glass*; it should be available in most principal libraries.

In *Canadian Interiors* in October, 1967, Mrs. Helen Ignatieff, then of the Sigmund Samuel Gallery of the Royal Ontario Museum, wrote that the glass made at Mallorytown was the "finest hand made glass to appear in the 19th century in Canada. For its useful function and decorative value it was never matched by any other glass manufactured here."

Perhaps. Certainly Mallorytown had supreme artists. The Mallorytown sweetmeat dish (Fig. 1) is one of the great pieces produced in Canada, but so is Jean Baptiste Machet's free blown flint glass footed pitcher (Fig. 6) as is the Burlington lamp (Fig. 51). Many of the whimseys are great works of art. Many Canadian artists produced very beautiful works in glass. Certainly, our early forebears at Mallorytown were, at a minimum, among the best.

If no one can question the beauty of the pieces made at Mallorytown, equally we must acknowledge its enormous importance in Canada's cultural history. From the perspective of the collector, the discovery and authentication of any piece of Mallorytown glass would be a major cultural contribution to Canada and a priceless discovery for the collector.

The serious collector should concentrate a search in widening circles from Mallorytown. My own procedure was to advertise, visit and interview. If a piece that is likely to be Mallorytown is found, it is very important to get signed statements from every person that knows anything about the piece.

Mallorytown glass is consistent in colour. Any departure from the colour of authenticated pieces should cause the collector to be very suspicious indeed; there would have to be overwhelming evidence before any colour variance, no matter how slight, could be accepted as Mallorytown. The glass works appears to have used the local White Potsdam sandstone and, as a consequence of the sandstone used, all authenticated pieces are consistently of a bluish green bottle-glass colour.

It is possible more pieces will be found. In an interview in 1954, Mrs. B. Ford Purvis told me of green-glass doorstops of a kind that had been in the district. Three years later I discovered a doorstop (Fig. 3) that was exactly the colour produced at Mallorytown and that fitted the description given by Mrs. Purvis. After examining the piece Mrs. Purvis wrote:

> "The green glass doorstop, with bits of white, blue and red glass inside, is the same as several used in old houses around Mallorytown, and the colour is exactly similar to that of a bottle obtained from the old glass works by Great Grandfather George Purvis."

The Mallorytown doorstop paperweight that is published here is to this date the only one known and authenticated. It is logical enough to expect that the artist who made one made more. Evidently he did. Mrs. Purvis has witnessed as to "several used in old houses" in the area in her time. I searched for them. Some later collector may succeed where I failed. Certainly, for the very serious collector, the search should not be viewed as hopeless. The consequence of a successful search would be to add to the few authenticated pieces now known to have been produced in Canada's earliest glass works.

FIGURE 1   *A free-blown, aquamarine-coloured ''Lily-Pad'' footed bowl. The bowl and applied base have folded rims. Five super-imposed ''Lily-Pad'' motifs. The base of the bowl reveals the scar of a pontil rod. Height 3³/8''; height of base 1¹/2''; diameter of bowl 5¹/2''; diameter of base 3³/16''. Mallorytown Glass Works, Canada West,* c. *1825-1839/40.*

FIGURE 2   *A free-blown, aquamarine-coloured milk bowl with folded rim and pontil mark on base. Height 4¹/4''; diameter at rim 10''; diameter at base 6³/4''. Mallorytown Glass Works, Canada West,* c. *1825-1839/40.*

FIGURE 3   *A doorstop paperweight with an aquamarine body containing a central bubble with small ruby, opal (milk white) and blue chips. Mallorytown Glass Works, Canada West,* c. *1825-1839/40.*

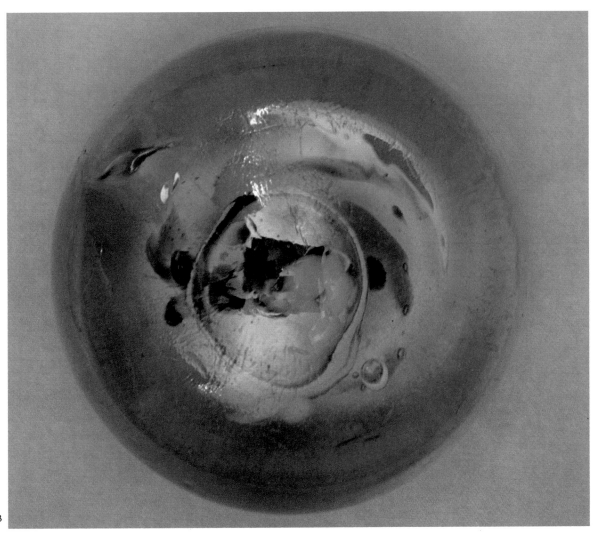

3

2 PAPERWEIGHTS

DINNER OVER, Gerald Stevens settled himself in his chair. Pieces of Canadian glass were on a table beside him. Heidi Redekop, Bea Stevens and I made ourselves comfortable, prepared to listen to one of Gerald's dissertations on Canadian glass.

Gerald picked up a piece of glass from the table beside him. It was a Baccarat-type pansy paperweight.

"For sheer beauty this may well be the finest paperweight ever made in Canada," said Gerald. "Did I ever tell you the story of finding and authenticating this piece?"

Heidi and I agreed he had not. Bea, who must have heard Gerald's stories many times before, merely smiled.

"Bea, will you get the pitcher and Edouard Machet's candlesticks and paperweight and Jean Baptist's other paperweight," asked Gerald.

"I'll grab a notebook," said Heidi. She frequently kept notes of Gerald's talks.

"These pieces were made by Jean Baptist Machet at the Excelsior Glass Company in Montreal, probably in the early 1880s," said Gerald, pointing to pitcher and paperweights.

He is probably Canada's greatest authenticated artist in glass.

I first became aware of Machet from a glassblower who had worked in the Diamond Glass Company in Montreal. I tried to trace back and was told that he had worked in the Diamond Glass Company in the 1890s. I was also told he had worked in the earlier Excelsior Glass Company in the early 1880s. There was a little confusion. But then I discovered that there were two Machets who had been early glassblowers. I later found that they were father and son.

I got interested: this kind of hint always brought out the latent detective in me. By phoning, making calls and in every other way I could think about I tried to locate a descendant of Jean Baptist Machet. On a happy day I found one and went to call on her.

You remember it, Bea?

I remember very well.

We found that Jean Baptist Machet was trained and worked as a glassblower in the famous Baccarat Glassworks in France. He had been persuaded by the Excelsior Glass Company to emigrate to Canada. He worked for many years in that plant as glassblower, artist and in the training of other workers in the glass techniques of Baccarat.

I asked if she had any of his work.

She came back with a glass bird form. It was swan-like, made of flint glass and seemed almost to be swimming with a living elan. It was decorated by wheel cut wings (see Fig. 7) and a carefully placed tear-drop-shaped bubble was floating in the solid body.

I knew at once I had not been misled. I was on the trail of a master artist.

When I left I had the swan. I also had a list of known relations of Machet. But my informant didn't know if any of them had glass pieces made by their artist antecedent.

It was a long list. Some whom I called on added new names. But I had real success. I found and authenticated a pair of glass candlesticks (Fig. 26) made by Edouard Machet—the son. He, like his father, had apprenticed at the Baccarat Glassworks in France.

Then, one day, I had the greatest day I have ever had in all my years of glass collecting or, with the exception of the day we discovered Mallorytown, in my years as a researcher.

I had the general location of relations of Jean Baptist Machet who lived in the East End of Montreal. They didn't seem to have any phone. I went out to try and find them.

It was a raw, slushy day in November. I had been late getting away, and then I couldn't find the place. I trudged up and down and finally found the street on which they were reported to live. But the number I'd been given wasn't to be found. The wind was raw and it went right through my coat as though it was cheese-cloth. It was getting dark. I was cold and discouraged. I decided to give it up. But as I was walking to find my car I made a last query of a man who was working on his car on the road. He knew them. Their house was at the back, behind the houses on the street.

It was a small place on an unlighted and muddy track. I was a little nervous as I knocked on the door.

A small woman answered. I told her I wanted to talk about Jean Baptist Machet.

"I just don't know," she said.

A voice bellowed from inside. "Who is it?"

"It's somebody about Jean Baptist."

"Well, tell him to come in or not! It's getting cold in here."

I walked in.

A coal-fired heating stove glowed on one side of the small room. A shirtless, hairy-chested man perspired beside it, a heavy roll of fat bulging out across his belt. The room was a drafty oven.

"What do you care about old Jean Baptist? He's dead. A long time now."

I was sitting on the edge of a chair, my coat still on in the hot room and my hat in my hand. I told him why I cared about Jean Baptist.

He didn't say anything as I talked. Then he questioned me pretty closely.

Finally he asked, "Is that stuff he made worth anything?"

I told him that it was.

He heaved himself out of his chair and disappeared into the lean-to kitchen. A moment later he was back with a frightening-looking butcher knife in his hand.

I moved closer to the edge of my chair! I marked my path to the door!

He went over to the middle of the room, got onto his knees, and poked at the linoleum. Finding a crack he cut three sides of a square through the linoleum, rolled it back, caught a ring and lifted a trapdoor in the floor.

"Get me my rubber boots."

He eased himself down and I heard the splash of water. He pushed a soggy wooden box onto the floor and climbed out after it. He pawed through wet paper and brought out a glass jug.

"May I see it?"

He handed it to me.

I was holding in my hands the work of a master artist in glass. It was a free-blown, footed pitcher with an applied handle (Fig. 6). The design was perfect.

A great piece of Canadiana had come from the water-logged hole beneath this East End home.

"Will you sell this?"

"Why not? Old Jean Baptist used to fiddle with that piece all the time when he came over, but he's past caring. Its been in the hole there for years. I'd forgotten about it."

"How much do you want?"

He looked at me craftily. "I'd look for a hundred dollars."

I scribbled out the history of the piece, as they told it, got both to sign it, and handed him five twenty dollar bills.

Maybe I was too excited to think. I clutched my new glass pitcher by the handle, shook hands all around and turned toward the door.

"There's another piece of old Jean Baptist's around here somewheres. D'you want that too?"

"What!"

Stevens the collector! Stevens the researcher! I was so excited at the one find I came close to walking out on another!

"What is it?"

"It's a lump of glass with flowers in it."

A paperweight! It had to be a paperweight!

They turned that little house upside down, and they couldn't find it.

"Somebody must have taken it. I guess its not here."

My original nervousness was long gone. "Let's all sit down, and both of you try and think where you last saw it."

"No good for me," said the man. "Last time I saw it was in the drawer in that thing over there. Ain't there now."

His wife sat silent. "My sister. I remember. She used it. She was mending socks. She pushed it in the toe . . . And I saw . . . I know where it is!"

In a moment she was back with a big box full of materials and mending. She rummaged into it.

"I knew it was there!"

In her work-marked hands she held a jewel of all jewels for the student, or researcher or collector of Canadian glass. She held a perfect Baccarat-style paperweight, the perfect pansy, the wheel cut base, the exquisite workmanship of a master craftsman (Fig. 9).

It no doubt was still slushy and muddy on the road. The wind may have been cutting when I walked back to my car with the paperweight and the Machet pitcher. If it was, I didn't notice.

So that is the story of my successful search for the story and the authentication of the glass of both Jean Baptist and Edouard Machet, Baccarat-trained, Canadian artisans of unparalleled skill. And I was able, through long work, to get other pieces from the family and fully authenticate them. I found the *Bottom of the Sea* paperweight by Jean Baptist (Fig. 9) and a very good Edouard Machet paperweight (Fig. 9), though there are flaws in Edouard's piece.

Gerald had finished his story. He turned again to the table and picked up a paperweight.

He started again: "Don't just get caught up in the find," he told us. "If I'd found any of the Machet pieces in a shop or at a show, they'd be just as beautiful and just as fine. But we wouldn't know who made them. We wouldn't be able to mark them as fully authenticated. They wouldn't have the same importance as a contribution to the heritage of Canada. They wouldn't be known as part of that heritage. But I became aware of the artists, I found their family members, I got authentication from each person from whom I collected these pieces, I went back with the pieces to other members of the family and double-checked. They are no more beautiful because of all that care, but they are now part of the official art records of Canada. The swan, jug and two paperweights were made by Jean Baptist Machet. The candlesticks and flawed paperweight were made by Edouard Machet. To have proved that is just as important as finding them."

"That's the way as collectors you also become useful researchers. With a piece that you see is important, ask the dealer where it came from, go and see those people. If they're not alive, trace their descendants. That's real collecting. Just to go out and buy only proves that you have the price of the piece. If a special piece is good enough to buy, it is good enough to be researched. You cannot get a great collection just with money, unless you have enough to buy somebody else's research and authentication. With important glass or furniture or guns or whatever, you must always go and trace the history of the piece just as far as you can—to the artisan that made it if you can."

"I hope you'll both always collect that way."

FIGURE 4   *This is an extremely rare "bird-on-pedestal" glass paperweight. It is quite possibly one-of-a-kind and was made from one gather of glass. The head, wings and tail were made by use of a pucellas and reveal the indented marks associated with this instrument and/or a spring tool. The base shows a large circular scar, resulting from the use of a pontil rod. Burlington Glass Works, Hamilton, Ontario, c. 1890.*

4

FIGURE 5   *On the left is a very interesting and relatively late swan paperweight. The colour and form are charming. The tail in particular suggests the late 19th century; it is, however, of the period* c. *1925-30.*

On the right is a Wallaceburg swan paperweight. Canadian bird paperweights and whimseys were a popular form of self expression and/or proof of skill among artisans in glass. This example was obtained in Wallaceburg and suggests influences emanating from Quebec.

The body is decorated with pale swirls of opal. The head, rudimentary wings and slightly elongated tail were achieved by the use of a pucellas or spring tool. These ever-present tools were indispensable, and the glass blower would have several sizes of each. Early bird forms, whether blown or solid, were given rudimentary wings and very short, decorative tails. This example was made in the Sydenham Glass Company, Wallaceburg, Ontario, c. *1895.*

5

FIGURE 6   *This spectacular free-blown, flint-glass, footed pitcher with applied handle was made by Jean Baptist Machet. The story of its rescue from a Montreal cellar is told on page 00. Rough pontil mark on base. Height 10³/₈″. The Excelsior Glass Company, Montreal, P.Q., c. 1881.*

6

FIGURE 7   *This rare bird form was made by the master glassworker, Jean Baptist Machet. It illustrates the use of a cutting wheel to suggest wings and the deliberate placement of a tear-drop bubble in the centre of the base. Note early tail. Length 3¾". Montreal, c. 1881.*

7

FIGURE 8 *Patrick Wickham was a glass blower who provided the collection of Canadian glass paperweights with a specific technique that is thought to be original. A Wickham weight has an aquamarine-coloured body within which floats a roughly formed, rectangular field of opal glass. The field bears a legend relative to the person for whom the weight was made. The data could include the given and/or family name, date, city, etc. The legend was written by the recipient using a lead pencil. The example on the left was made for "Lizzie Wilkes 1895," while the weight on the right was created for "Miss Lily Brown, Toronto, Ont." Both were made by Wickham at the Toronto Glass Company which was in business from 1894-1900.*

FIGURE 9 *Jean Baptist Machet made the "Baccarat" paperweight shown in the top centre while working at the Excelsior Glass Company, Montreal, c. 1881. The body is of lead glass obtained in the Excelsior factory, and the "set-ups" were brought from the "Baccarat" glass factory in France.*

The important example of a "made in Canada" paperweight shown on the left was also created by Jean Baptist Machet, circa *1892. The title of this item is* Bottom of the Sea, *inspired by a coral reef surmounted by seaweed. The body of the weight is of lead glass. The motif is of finely broken opal glass, and the "seaweed" is of a green glass used to manufacture coal oil lamps of the period.*

On the right is a Lily-in-Flowerpot *paperweight made by Edouard Machet at the Diamond Glass Company, Montreal, c. 1895.*

Relative to the subject of lead glass made in Canada, the "Diamond Flint Glass Company Limited, Lamp Chimney Catalogue and Price List" contains thirty-seven entries for "Pure Vulcan Lead." This answers the many questions concerning the ability of Canadian glass makers to produce lead glass.

8

FIGURE 10   *On the left is a weight that provides proof relative to the Canadian glassblower's knowledge and use of sulphides. In this instance, the French-Canadian glass blower could have used a crucifix from a rosary to create a mould into which the ceramic mixture could be poured. The firing could have resulted from the heat available in the glory hole. Sydenham Glass Company, Wallaceburg, Ontario, 1910. On the right is shown a crucifix (sulphide) paperweight obtained from the reverend gentleman for whom it was made. Sydenham Glass Company, Wallaceburg, Ontario, c. 1909.*

10

FIGURE 11 *The Hamilton Glass Works, Hamilton, Ontario, flourished from 1865 to 1895. It was a ''container house'' and manufactured mould-blown bottles, containers (fruit jars) and ''Bogardus'' balls (glass balls used by 19th century trap-shooters). The type of paperweight shown here, with its medium aquamarine-blue body containing small round and teardrop-shaped bubbles, was very popular with the Hamilton glassblowers, and specimens have been found which vary from standard to extremely large. This example dates from* c. *1885.*

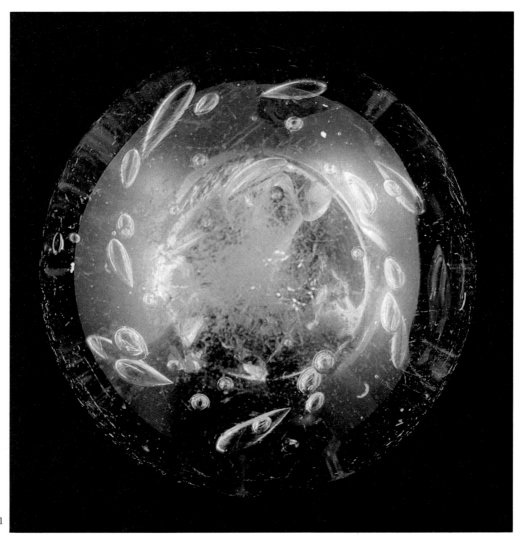

11

FIGURE 12 *In the upper left is a pressed and stained commercial weight made at the Toronto Glass Company Toronto, Ontario, c. 1894-1900. See Early Canadian Glass, p. 83. On the right is a pressed-glass, semi-commercial paperweight produced at the Diamond Glass Company, Montreal, P.Q., c. 1890-1902. The crucifix paperweight at the lower left has a clear glass body containing a crude cross made from two rounded pieces of opal glass. In addition, there are swirls of a transparent green colour suggesting that the batch of glass was destined for the cullet pile. When acquired the weight was in excellent condition. However, when Mrs. Stevens and I were examining it, the person from whom it was obtained stated that the weight could not be broken, and, snatching it from our hands, threw it on the flagstone porch. The resultant break was clean, making it possible to obtain photographs of the weight's interior. The piece came from the Canada Glass Company, Hudson, P.Q., c. 1870.*

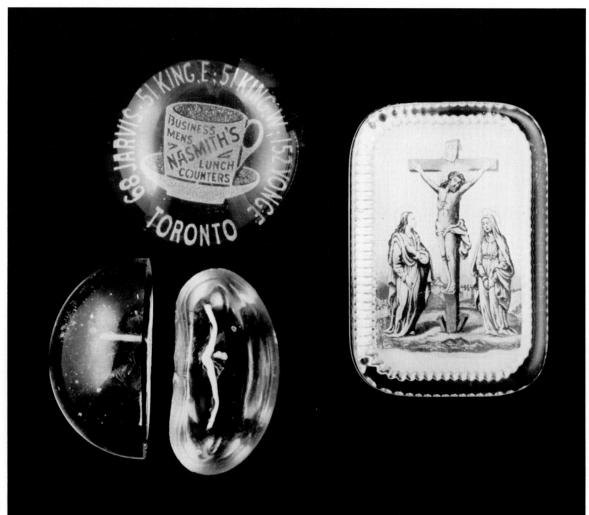

12

FIGURE 13   *A group of four paperweights associated with the Burlington Glass Works, Hamilton, Ontario.*

The piece in the upper left is typical of this type, with its field of multi-coloured chips, but the field includes the unusual feature of a number of custard-coloured chips obtained from damaged pressed and mould-blown tableware.

The "Burlington" weight in the upper right has an interesting "petal" design in cranberry glass enclosed in clear, flint glass. The uneven

shard of opal which reveals the date of manufacture (1894), was numbered by means of a pencil.

The interesting design in the lower left was achieved by the use of strips of opal glass forming a background for chips coloured ruby, deep blue and opal.

Another typical "Burlington" paperweight is shown in the lower right. The field consists of chips coloured ruby, medicine-bottle blue and white opal.

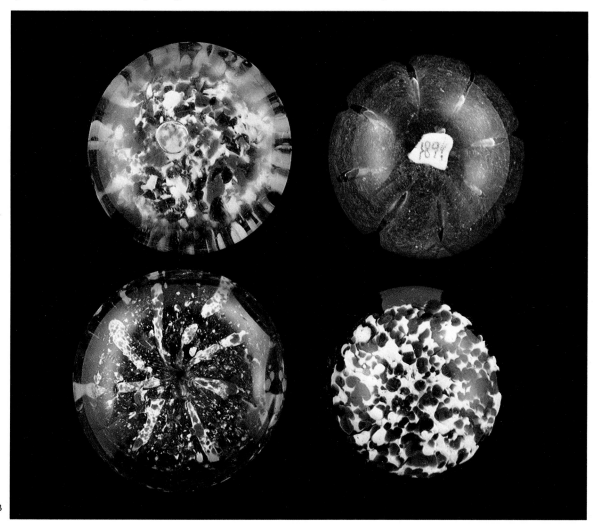

13

FIGURE 14 *The "Mrs. J. Watson" weight in the lower right is an interesting example of a type produced in some numbers. They were non-commercial and made in the Diamond Flint Glass Company, Montreal, P.Q., c. 1910. Each one was approximately similar in size and motifs, the one exception being the name of the person for whom the weight was made. These were presentation paperweights and were most difficult to obtain.*

The "H. Moses" and "John L. Ripley" weights are somewhat similar to the preceding example. They are, however, of a larger size, and there are many variants in the decorative motifs. The single colour of the excellently fragmented blue field in the Ripley weight is relatively unusual in Canadian glass. These two pieces also originated in the Diamond Flint Glass Company, Montreal, c. 1890-1902.

14

FIGURE 15 *This group of four paperweights illustrates the use of a name of a recipient inside the glass. The "E. Lafferty" example (upper left) was made by George Mullin about 1890. See* Early Canadian Glass, *p. 45, and* Canadian Glass c. 1825-1925, *facing p. 20. This is an extremely rare example of a weight signed by the maker. The extremely small initials "GM" are to be found on the large piece of opal (milk) glass immediately below the "LA" in Lafferty. Mullin worked in the Burlington Glass Works, Hamilton, Ontario, which operated between 1875 and 1909.*

George Mullin also made the "Jno. B. Watt" weight shown in the upper right at about the same period of time. See Early Canadian Glass, *p. 45. Mr. Watt was President of the Toronto Glass Company, Toronto, Ontario, from 1894 to 1900.*

George Gardiner authenticated the example of a sulphide paperweight illustrated in the lower left. Sulphides were produced in several Canadian glass factories, and the name refers to three dimensional ceramic forms used as internal decorations in paperweights and alleys.

The ceramic bird used in this "P. B. Fetterley, London, Ontario" weight provides proof that Canadian glass blowers knew and used this technique. The skilled maker was Billy McGinnis, the "gaffer" or head of a shop of glass blowers. See Canadian Glass c. 1825-1925, *facing p. 20.*

The "Wm. Benedict" example in the lower right reveals modifications of design and colour, and it illustrates the use of an uncoloured sulphide form.

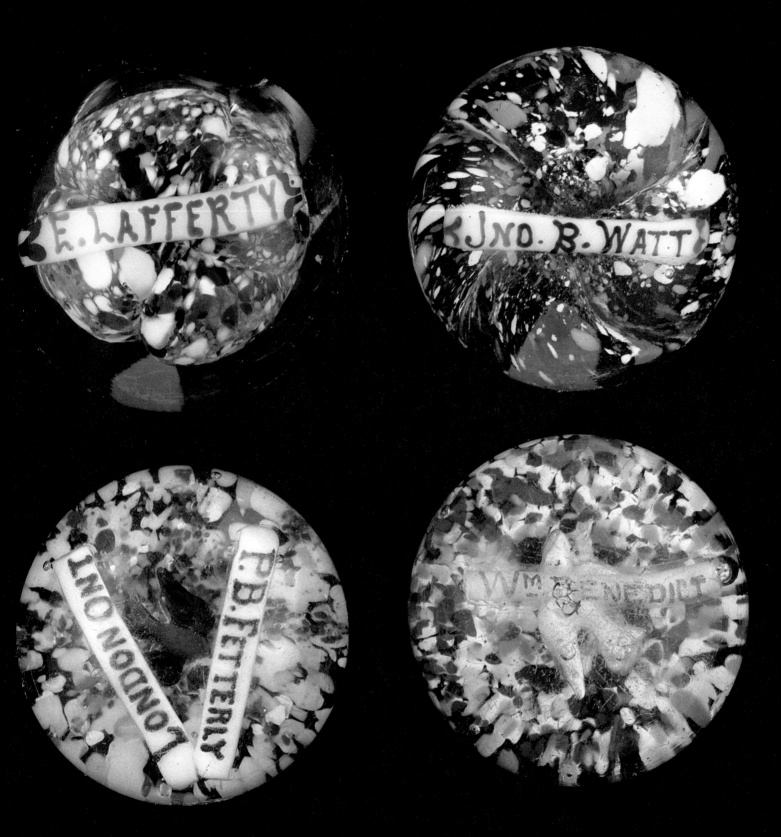

FIGURE 16 *All of these paperweights were made in the Burlington Glass Works, Hamilton, Ontario, between 1875 and 1909.*

The examples in the upper left and lower right are George Gardiner-type weights which may or may not have been made by him c. 1895.

The piece in the lower left has been authenticated as a paperweight made by George Gardiner in the Burlington Glass Works, 1898. Height 3¹/₈"; circumference 10¹/₈". The ground consists of multi-coloured chips, and the motif is a cased glass, five-petalled lily growing from a bubble stem. The petals are of opal glass overlaid with emerald green. See Canadian Glass c. 1825-1925, *facing p. 20.*

The weight in the upper right has a similar lily and bubble stem. The triangular arrangement of opal glass bears the legend: "Mr. Geo. Patterson—437 Catherine—Hamilton, Ont. 1908. Although this weight has been badly damaged and much of the base is missing, it still shows the typical Burlington field of coloured chips.

FIGURE 17 *A group of five paperweights made at the Diamond Glass Company, Montreal, P.Q., which was open for business between 1890 and 1902.*

The example in the upper left is a form of "non-commercial" Montreal weight said to have been sold to the public.

The "Good Luck" weight provides documentation for several other examples that were produced c. 1900.

In the centre is an interesting form of sentimental glass weight that was made in some numbers.

In the lower left is an example of the kind of paperweight presented to fraternal societies. The legends, motifs and field of multi-coloured chips are typical of this specific form of Canadian glass paperweight. For an extended discussion of this piece, see Early Canadian Glass, *p. 131.*

The motif and legends contained in the piece shown in the lower right are made from very finely fragmented opal glass. This design was produced in some numbers and is said to have been presented to the fraternal society documented in the glass. The field consists of a multiplicity of coloured chips, several of which suggest further potential for the study of the use of colour in early Canadian glass factories.

16

FIGURE 18 *A group of five weights made at the Sydenham Glass Company, Wallaceburg, Ontario, which flourished from 1895 to 1910.*

The interesting piece shown in the upper left documents the close co-operation between the glassblowing fraternities of Ontario and Quebec. The weight is of the five-petal lily with bubble stem concept. The legends are of blue on rectangular opal fields. The field is of opal chips supporting a five-petalled design of chips coloured blue, pale blue, yellow and pink. Made in 1910 for Arthur Leonard by Albany Leonard, his brother. See Canadian Glass c. 1825-1925, *facing p. 20. Fifteen years earlier Albany Leonard, then employed at the Diamond Glass Company in Montreal, made the free-blown bird shown in Figure 28, also illustrated in* Canadian Glass c. 1825-1925, p. 51. *The Leonard brothers, Albany, Arthur and Joseph, received their training and worked at the Diamond Glass Company in Montreal, later all transferring to Wallaceburg.*

The weight created for "J. Gasnell" (c. 1900) has a multi-coloured field enclosed in flint glass. The legend is in cobalt blue on a strip of opal. As was the custom of Canadian makers of non-commercial paperweights, the base of this presentation piece reveals the scar resulting from the use of a pontil rod.

In the centre is a paperweight containing a five-petalled lily of ruby glass and an air-bubble stem. The legend "William Sharpe Ridgetown" appears at the base of the stem; it is of blue on a triangle of opal strips. The triangle rests on a field of multi-coloured chips.

The recipient of the "Emma" paperweight illustrated in the lower left was a niece of the maker. The legend was written on a shard of blue opal, and the field is of chips coloured ruby, medicine-bottle blue and white opal. Circa 1899.

The ground of the "Dr. G. Covel" weight shown in the lower right consists of five joined mounds of opal glass upon the crests of which are scattered glass chips of pale blue, deep blue, ruby, yellow and pink. The legend is in cobalt on a strip of white opal. Circa 1912. See Canadian Glass c. 1825-1925, *facing p. 20*

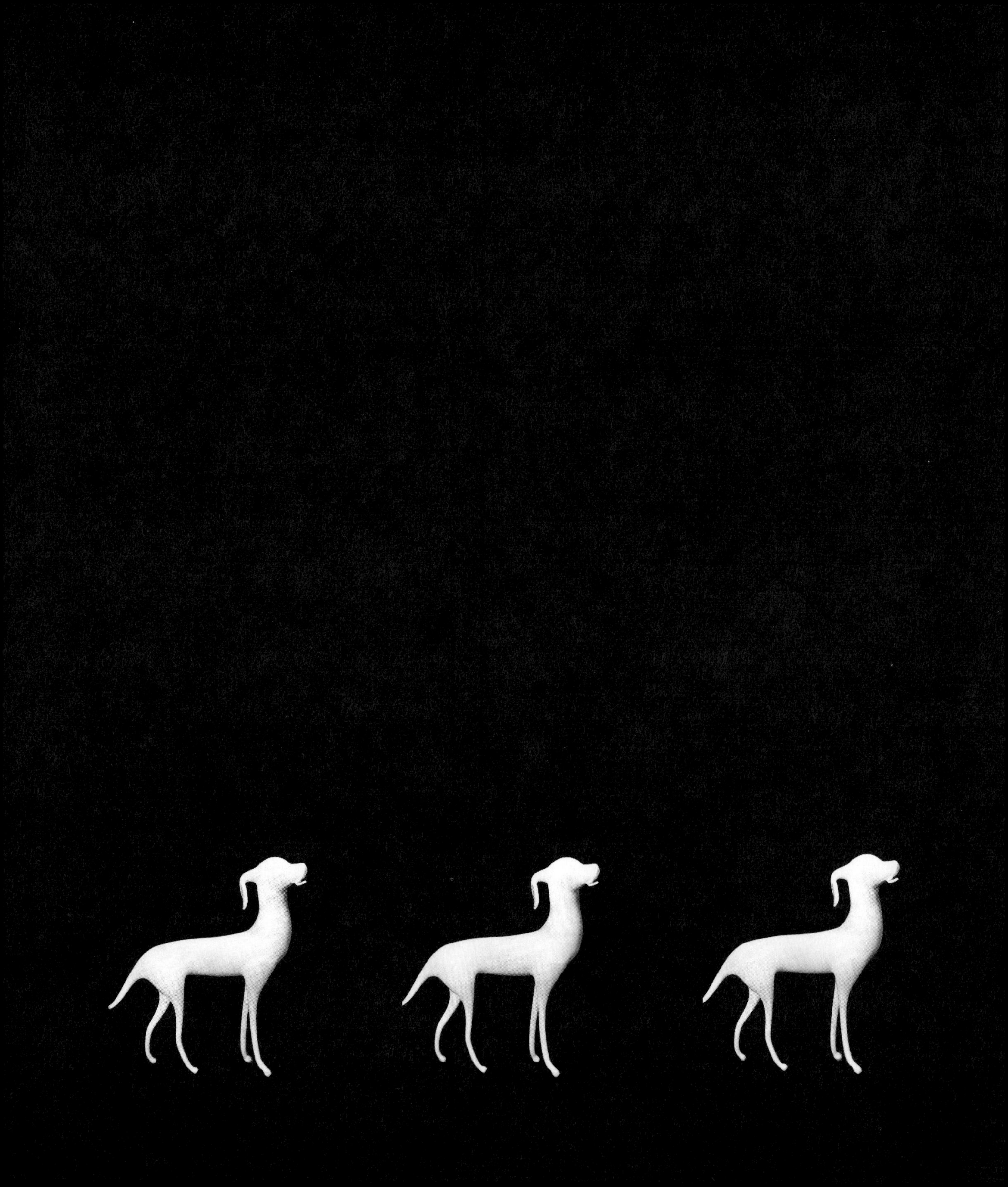

3 WHIMSEYS

THIS IS AN INTERVIEW between George Gardiner of Hamilton, Ontario, and Gerald Stevens. The place is the home of Mr. Gardiner. The time is October 31, 1958.

At that time, Mr. Gardiner was one of the few surviving 19th century Canadian glassblowers. He began his career in the Burlington Glass House, Hamilton, Ontario, in 1885. He retired from the trade in 1915, by which time the ancient art of glassblowing and manipulation by means of blow pipe and punty rod were superseded by mechanical methods.

G.S.: Mr. Gardiner, at what age did you join the Burlington Glass Works?

G.G.: Eleven years old.

G.S.: What was your first work?

G.G.: Carrying-in fruit jars to the annealing ovens.

G.S.: Was there any particular name for the boys who did that?

G.G.: Yes, the carrying-in-boy.

G.S.: At what age did you become an apprentice?

G.G.: Twenty-three years.

G.S.: What were your duties as an apprentice?

G.G.: We were blowing fruit jars and bottles.

G.S.: How long did you serve as an apprentice before becoming a qualified glassblower?

G.G.: Five years.

G.S.: What were your duties during that period? Were you blowing glass all the time?

G.G.: Yes, we were blowing glass; blowing fruit jars and bottles.

G.S.: Was an apprentice given special training, or did he just pick it up as he went along?

G.G.: No, he was generally instructed by the other glassblowers in the factory.

G.S.: Any particular hour or time, or just while the work went on?

G.G.: Just while the work went on.

G.S.: We know the glassblowers were, and I quote from an address by Mr. D. A. Hayes, president of the union, "the aristocracy of labour." This being so, what pay did the glassblower of the 1890s receive?

G.G.: $9 - $10 a day.

G.S.: Was that the general rate of pay?

G.G.: Well, from $6 up.

G.S.: What caused the difference in rate of pay ranging from $6 to $10?

G.G.: Some of the bottles paid more than the other ones. We always worked according to our lists.

G.S.: Was the rate of pay based on the weekly, hourly or piece work rate?

G.G.: All piece work.

G.S.: What would be the daily production of a qualified glassblower, working on piece work? How many could you produce in a single day?

G.G.: In the small shop that I worked we made the small ones, about five hundred dozen a day.

G.S.: By one man?

G.G.: No, by three. It took three men to constitute a shop.

G.S.: I see, a grouping of three constituted a shop, and a factory would constitute many shops. How many glassblowers would be working, on average, in your time at Burlington?

G.G.: About sixty.

G.S.: Glass collectors are always interested in whimseys and the little special pieces that glassblowers made. When did the glassblowers find time to make pieces for themselves or their friends?

G.G.: During lunch hour.

G.S.: They didn't do any work after hours or anything like that— always during lunch hours?

G.G.: Yes, all lunch hours.

G.S.: Were the factories going twenty-four hours a day?

G.G.: Yes.

G.S.: How long was a shift?

G.G.: Eight hours.

G.S.: You are represented in a collection of Canadian glass in the

Royal Ontario Museum by several pieces including a drape and a paperweight. How were these made?

G.G.: Well, the paperweight was quite a thing to make. You had to have the different colours of glass. You broke them up on an iron plate. Then you dipped your punty and gathered the glass and rolled it into the coloured glass. You took the other glass out of the furnace and moulded it with a wooden block. After that you took some coloured glass in and you worked it and shaped it. Then when you wanted to put the lilies in it you put the five pieces of glass out front and got your glass hot. You would put the glass over the five leaves. Then you took a compass and you pierced it in the hot glass. That made the lily. After that you covered it up again and you moulded it again and you rolled it and rolled it until it got the desired shape. Then by sticking the compass in and pulling it out quick— why, then that formed the lily and the bubble in the lily.

G.S.: By sticking the compass into the glass, it is really an air pocket you were putting in the glass? That is why it looks silvery?

G.G.: Yes.

G.S.: The drape illustrates many techniques used in glassmaking, such as cake glass, candy cane and others. How were these special effects obtained?

G.G.: Well, I would have coloured glass and I would put it in the furnace. I would watch it while it would melt. Then I would get it on my punty, roll it, pull it out and then make a link. As a rule I used to make so many links every night till I got the quantity I wanted—red, white, blue, amber and so on.

G.S.: Some of them were cast glass with colour, such as blue or red, covered with clear glass?

G.G.: Yes. I threw the colour in there and covered it over with the plain glass.

G.S.: By putting the coloured glass into the clear glass it incorporated itself into the bath of metal in the melting pot?

G.G.: Yes.

G.S.: How did you make the candy cane where it was twisted, clear glass with a centre of red, white and blue drawn out and twisted?

G.G.: That was started with the coloured glass being on the iron plate. I'd take a piece of clear glass out of the furnace and roll it into the colour until it got round. Then you would put it in the furnace, then roll it again. Then we'd take a pair of pinchers and put it over a snap. We called it a snap, used for holding bottles when they used to put them in the furnace to put the ring on the neck. We would take the pinchers and twist, and then we'd wrap it around the snap. Then when we got what we wanted, we would nip it off with a pair of shears and then shape it.

G.S.: This snap, what type of thing was that?

G.G.: Just a piece of round iron, steel.

G.S.: How long would it be?

G.G.: About four inches.

G.S.: Then it would have a long wooden handle?

G.G.: No, an iron handle.

G.S.: Could you hold it? Wouldn't the handle become too hot?

G.G.: No, no, we could hold it.

G.S.: Mr. Gardiner, could you describe other types of whimseys made by the glassblowers?

G.G.: Glass hats, glass hammers, glass hatchets, glass bells, canes, umbrella handles.

G.S.: Could you describe one of the glass bells?

G.G.: Well, there was one man in the factory, his name is George Mullin, and he was an artist at making a glass bell. George made the bell by taking the glass out of the furnace and blowing a bubble and opening it up with a pair of tools. Then he'd flare it till he got it the shape of a bell.

G.S.: What about the handle?

G.G.: He put the handle on after. It was applied.

G.S.: I've seen some with clappers in them, to ring the bell.

G.G.: Oh yes, you mean the knockers. Well, I've seen George make one. I don't know whether it would ring or not, but he had one in there anyway. Of course it was lime glass, it wasn't lead. If it was lead, it would have rung.

G.S.: You speak of lime and lead glass. What were the different types of glass used in Burlington and Toronto?

G.G.: In Hamilton when they used to make salt and pepper shakers they used an opal glass. White, blue. The other things were all lime glass or lead glass.

G.S.: What is the difference between lime glass and lead glass?

G.G.: The lead glass you could make anything you liked. Some like Mr. Mullin used to make the bells. If you made it out of lime glass and put the knockers inside, why it would not ring. If it was made out of lead glass, it would have made a good sound.

G.S.: There is a greater resonance to lead glass?

G.G.: Yes.

G.S.: Was lead glass made in great quantity here in Hamilton?

G.G.: No, now and again they'd get an order for a batch of lamp chimneys and such. Some of them would want them to be made out of lead glass.

G.S.: Lead glass was only made on special order?

G.G.: That's right.

G.S.: What were some of the names of the best of the glassblowers? You mentioned George Mullin. What are the names of some of the others that were outstanding?

G.G.: Well there was Billy McGinnis, Nick Daley. They were really artists with a piece of glass, too.

G.S.: I've heard you mention Pat Wickham.

G.G.: Pat Wickham. He was good. Good on paperweights too.

G.S.: Where had these men received their training?

G.G.: Well, mostly they had their training over in the States in the early years. There are a number of Canadians right here in Canada who turned out just as good a thing as they ever did in the States.

G.S.: Did any of these special glassblowers or men that you knew start any glass factories of their own?

G.G.: Yes, the Foster brothers started one over in Port Colborne.

G.S.: Were they real glass houses where they melted the glass from basic materials, or did they use cullet and that sort of thing?

G.G.: They used the basic materials, and they also used quite a bit of cullet. But in Port Colborne they were pretty near all fruit jars. That was their general output.

G.S.: I can remember you telling me about someone who would go out to the dump and pick up old broken glass and bottles who tried to operate a glass house in that manner. Can you remember who that was, Mr. Gardiner?

G.G.: Yes, I remember, but the poor fellow is dead now. He started a glass house out in Dundas. But it never materialized.

G.S.: What was his name?

G.G.: Whittaker. Jim Whittaker. I think his name was Jim Whittaker. He had two boys, and they worked here together with Mr. Whittaker when they were making lamp chimneys. They worked at the shop. The two boys and the father.

G.S.: They were working at the shop in Burlington?

G.G.: The Burlington Glass Works in Hamilton.

G.S.: They didn't stay in business? Did they make any glass at all?

G.G.: Yes. I and a friend of mine went out there looking at some of the glass that they had made, and it was full of blisters. It was the effect of using too much cullet.

G.S.: Would that cause the bubbles and blisters in Mexican glass that we see today?

G.G.: It could.

G.S.: What were they trying to make? What shapes or forms?

G.G.: They were trying to make bottles.

G.S.: And fruit jars?

G.G.: No, I don't remember them making fruit jars.

G.S.: Do you remember the date of this venture?

G.G.: Yes, I may be mistaken, but I got a good idea that it was fifty years ago [1908].

G.S.: Mr. Gardiner, what factories did you work in other than the Burlington glasshouse?

G.G.: Well, I worked in Hamilton, I worked in Toronto, I worked in New York, Indiana, Illinois and I worked in Wisconsin.

G.S.: Did you work in Wallaceburg, too?

G.G.: Oh yes. I did work in Wallaceburg, too. I forgot that.

G.S.: Were the methods of glassmaking and blowing used by these other houses that you worked in similar to those used in Burlington?

G.G.: Yes, they were about the same.

G.S.: In other words, if you could make a piece of glass or come up to the qualifications necessary in Burlington, you could blow glass anywhere?

G.G.: Yes, that's right. You could blow glass from Montreal to San Francisco.

G.S.: Mr. Gardiner, what were glassblowers like as individuals?

G.G.: Well, a good hard-working bunch. They made good money, but they didn't hang on to it. That is the only fault they had, the only fault I could see with them. They made it, and they distributed it, plenty.

G.S.: What types of things did they distribute it on?

G.G.: Well, mostly they were good sports. They were always there for a baseball game, or cock fights and even a dog fight. They always had plenty on. They would bet on them. Certainly they'd bet, they'd bet their shirts.

G.S.: It is suggested that 19th century glassblowers were particularly heavy imbibers. Is this based on fact?

G.G.: No, it is not. There were a few, the odd one, but you could find them in any trade. But they were not, they were a fine bunch of men. Anyway, if they drank too much the night before, they wouldn't last long in the glasshouse. The heat was intense and they could not have stood it.

G.S.: What degree of heat would there be in the glasshouse?

G.G.: Sometime I used to think it was about five thousand. I guess it was around a hundred.

G.S.: It would be very difficult to work in surroundings like that during the heat of the summer? Did the glasshouse ever close down during a heat wave?

G.G.: No, we always slowed down at the end of June. We went until then unless the tank should happen to spring a leak. Then it'd burn out, and we'd have to look for another job to finish off the season. We always took our holidays in July and August.

G.S.: In general the glasshouses closed during July and August? Did Burlington?

G.G.: Yes.

G.S.: It has been suggested that glassblowers could arrange a day off whenever they wished?

G.G.: It could be arranged all right, by throwing a handful of nails or a file in a pot of glass. When that was done that glass would have to be ladled out and a fresh lot put in.

G.S.: Why would it have to be ladled out? What would the iron do to the glass batch?

G.G.: You couldn't control it on your pipe with the iron in there. The glass would not stay on the pipe when it was mixed in with iron.

G.S.: There were two glasshouses in Hamilton. One is the Burlington glasshouse and the other is the Hamilton Glass Works. What type of glass objects did the Hamilton Glass Works manufacture?

G.G.: They made fruit jars, bottles, and one part of them, they made what they call a twister bottle. That is when you put the glass in the bottle mould, and they kept turning the pipe in their mouth. When they took the bottle out of the mould, well, they had no seam on it.

G.S.: You couldn't see the mould seams?

G.G.: No.

G.S.: Did they make lamp chimneys and tableware, that sort of thing?

G.G.: No, not in the Hamilton Glass Works.

G.S.: The Burlington Glass Works made glass in every form? You mentioned that they made salts and peppers.

G.G.: They made salts and peppers, tableware, lamps and they made fruit dishes, other things. All kinds of dishes. They also made bird cups. They made candy jars.

G.S.: What shapes were these candy jars?

G.G.: All kinds. Some of them were made in the shape of a revolver.

G.S.: The revolvers . . . . I understand that they made them from clear glass. They were hollow and were filled with candy and closed with tin screw-tops on the muzzle?

G.G.: Yes, that's right.

FIGURE 19 *Three free-blown pieces. On the left is flint-glass bowl with a rough pontil mark on the base (height 6"). In the centre is a free-blown, non-commercial drinking glass with expanded lip and pontil mark. Height 5½". On the right is a flint-glass bowl with a rough pontil mark on the base (height 4⅛".) The Diamond Glass Company, Montreal, c. 1900.*

FIGURE 20 *This free-blown druggist's jar is decorated with two applied rings of solid glass. The finial is circular and stepped. Made in a two-piece mould. Originally authenticated by Edith Chown Pierce. Height 8⅞"; diameter 5¾"; cover height 3⅞". See* The Canadian Collector, *p. 20. Napanee Glass Works, Napanee, Ontario, c. 1881-1883.*

20

19

FIGURE 21 *A flock of very interesting bird-form whimseys. From left to right: a solid, three-dimensional form 2³/8″ in height; a rare, free-blown whimsey 4″ in height (cp. Fig. 28); a bird form with early tail 4¹/4″ in length; and on the far right a rare bird form (see Fig. 7) that illustrates the use of a cutting wheel to suggest wings and a deliberately placed tear-drop bubble in the centre of the base— length 3³/4″. This last piece was made by Jean Baptist Machet at The Excelsior Glass Company, Montreal, c. 1891.*

FIGURE 22 *Another flock of bird-form whimseys. All except the one on the far left have rudimentary wings. From left to right: length 1³/4″, length 2″, length 1³/4″, length 1¹/2″; centre foreground, length 1³/4″.*

21

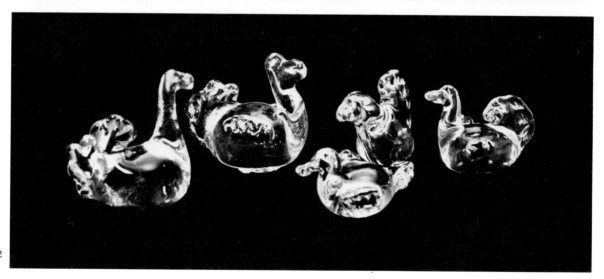

22

FIGURE 23 *Four free-blown glass-bell whimseys. From left to right: a flint bell with clapper, height 7³⁄₄", Montreal, P.Q., c. 1895; a glass bell, height 6", Montreal, c. 1910; a flint glass bell with clapper, height 7³⁄₄", Montreal, c. 1895; a glass bell made of "Crown Fine Flint," height 6³⁄₈", Burlington Glass Works, Hamilton, Ontario, c. 1900. This last piece was made from a blown lamp chimney, also at Burlington.*

23

FIGURE 24   *This is an interesting example of a semi-commercial, free-blown, footed bowl with a bird-form finial on the cover. An excellent quality of non-lead, flint glass was used by the glass-blower. The cover and foot reveal the smoothly ground scars that indicate the use of a pontil rod, while the crest and tail of the bird reveal the use of a spring tool. The period c. 1915 is suggested by the bird's elongated tail.*

24

FIGURE 25 *Four bird-form whimseys. From left to right: length 5½", length 5¼", length 3½", height 2¼". The clear glass bird second from left is interesting, because the length of the neck and tail suggest later manufacture, perhaps* c. *1910. There is a teardrop bubble in the central area of the base, with a rough pontil mark directly below it.*

FIGURE 26 *The free-blown glass pipe on the left (length approx. 12") was made in Trenton, Nova Scotia,* c. *1912.*

Next to it is a free-blown glass fishing float used with rod and line. Length 5¼". Burlington Glass Works, Hamilton, Ontario, c. *1909.*

Edouard Machet made the free-blown glass candlestick and solid candle with pontil mark. This may be unique. The rarity of 19th century glass candles and candlesticks is such that the combination is unlisted in any publication known to the author. Length of candlestick 5¼"; length of candle 8⅛". Diamond Glass Company, Montreal, P.Q., c. *1895.*

The free-blown glass pipe at the far right (length 11¾") was made in Montreal, c. *1910.*

FIGURE 27 *In the background of this illustration are a free-blown rolling pin whimsey and a flint-glass potato masher. The rolling pin is in aquamarine-coloured glass. Length 15". Hamilton Glass Works, Hamilton, Ontario,* c. *1890. The potato masher was free blown. Length 9". Hamilton Glass Works,* c. *1895.*

In the foreground (left to right) is a group of clear-glass whimseys. The small, mould-blown commercial perfume bottle (length 3") was excavated on the site of the Burlington Glass Works, Hamilton, Ontario; made c. *1895. Revolver bottles similar to the one shown were made by glassblowers to brandish during Labour Day parades; when used commercially they were filled with coloured candies and sold to children of all ages. See* Early Canadian Glass, *p. 60. The small, free-blown medicine bottle (height 3⅝") shown standing in this photograph was excavated at the Burlington Glass Works site; manufactured* c. *1895. The free-blown, flint-glass sock darner (length 5¼") on the far right was made at the Diamond Glass Company, Montreal, P.Q.,* c. *1899.*

26

25

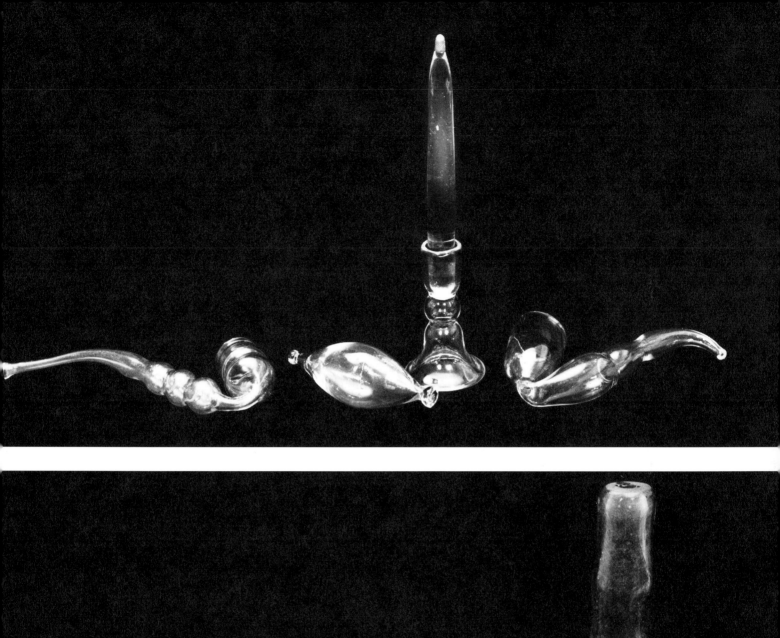

FIGURE 28 *This "one-of-a-kind," free-blown bird form is relatively large: height 5¹/₈″, length 7¹/₈″. The body is hollow and reveals a circular blow-pipe scar. The head, rudimentary wings and tail provide evidence that the maker used a pucellas and/or a spring tool. The tail has been touched with red paint, and the hollow interior has been filled with paper coloured red, green, yellow, blue and purple. The tail is an early form, the date is* c. *1895. Blown by Albany Leonard at the Diamond Glass Company, Montreal. Albany Leonard, subsequently employed in the Sydenham Glass Factory, Wallaceburg, Ontario, also made the "Souvenir de Wallaceburg" paperweight illustrated in Figure* 18.

28

FIGURE 29 *The very rare bird form on the left is a paperweight. The body is decorated with multi-coloured, finely ground chips. The dark green piece in the centre is the same colour as that used in making the green Bull's-Eye coal-oil lamps popular with collectors of Canadian glass. Length 5⅛". The ''container green'' bird on the right has a rough pontil mark on the base. The head and elongated tail were shaped with a pucellas. Length 4½". Burlington Glass Works, Hamilton, Ontario, c. 1890.*

29

FIGURE 30 *A very interesting whimsey that could be one of a kind. This machine-made milk bottle (mould seams extend to the top area of the lip) was found in Napanee, Ontario. It was cut by an expert trained in working on lead glass, who cut floral motifs on non-lead glass to exhibit his skill. Cut* circa *1915-1925.*

FIGURE 31 *The top three pieces in this illustration represent the glass blower's concept of the well known policeman's baton or nightstick; they date from the period* c. *1892. The whimsey at the bottom of the photograph resembles a baton but is, however, meant to be a personalized pestle to be used in the home; it dates from* c. *1900. All four originated in the Diamond Glass Company, Montreal, P.Q.*

The example at the top is made of solid glass decorated with one deliberately placed bubble. The tip and base of the handle show pontil scars; length 12¹/₄″. The whimsey below it is a similar nightstick form; length 7⁵/₈″. The third baton is an extremely rare, hollow, blown baton with interior decoration of finely ground chips of opal glass; length 6¹/₂₈. The pestle has a ground pontil mark; length 6³/₈″.

FIGURE 32 *These hammer and hatchet whimseys all date from the period* c. *1890-1895.*

The pale green, off-hand hammer in the upper left has a blown, applied handle, a pontil mark on the head and a blow-pipe opening in the handle. Length 8¹/₈″. Trenton, Nova Scotia, c. *1890.*

The rare, honey-amber coloured hammer in the upper right reveals pontil scars on the head and handle. The handle has been applied to the head. Length 8¹/₄″. Montreal, P.Q., c. *1895.*

The smaller, off-hand, clear glass hammer in the lower left has an applied handle and head showing ground pontil marks. Length 5¹/₂″. Montreal, c. *1890.*

The hatchet in the centre foreground is a rare off-hand, blown flint-glass example. The head is solid with a ground pontil mark. The applied handle terminates in an open, circular scar indicating the use of a blow pipe. Length 9³/₄″, height 4¹/₈″. The Excelsior Glass Company, Montreal, P.Q., c. *1891.*

The edge and head of the off-hand, clear-glass hatchet in the lower foreground were ground on a wheel. The applied handle has a ground pontil mark. Length 9¹/₂″. Montreal, c. *1895.*

31

30

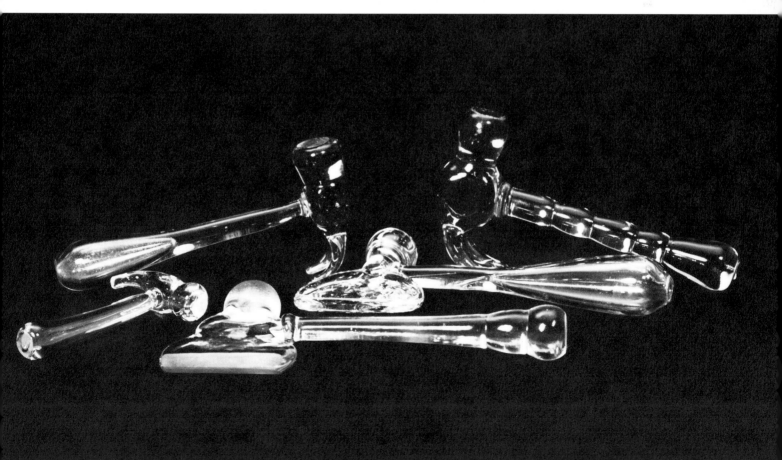

FIGURE 33 *The interesting example of a free-blown, flint-glass rolling pin was made by George Gardiner, c. 1890. The hollow interior was coated with extremely minute, fragmented granules or multi-coloured glass. Burlington Glass Works, Hamilton, Ontario.*

In the left foreground is a mould-blown "Bogardus" ball (a "pigeon" used in trap-shooting). It carries the embossed legend "Gurd & Son, 185 Dundas Street, London, Ontario." Circumference 8⅞". This very rare piece was made in the Hamilton Glass Works, Hamilton, Ontario, c. 1870. See Canadian Glass c. 1825-1925, *p. 12.*

In the right foreground is a honey amber witch ball. Circumference 13½". See Early Canadian Glass, *p. 44. Burlington Glass Works, Hamilton, c. 1895.*

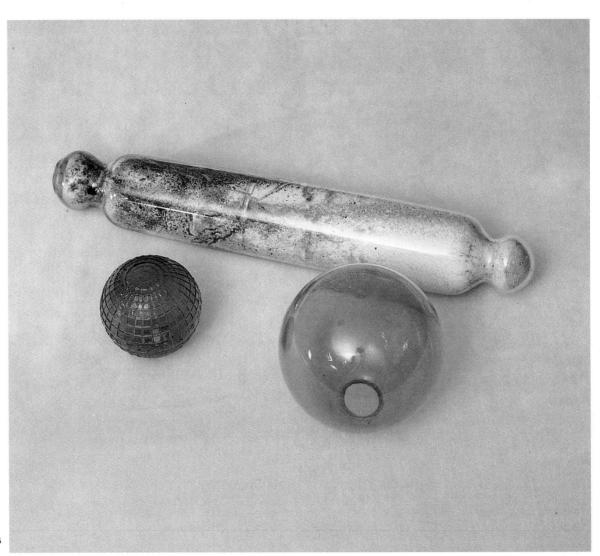

33

FIGURE 34 *In the upper left and upper right are deep amber cornucopia whimseys. These fragile items were made by the use of a blow-pipe and pucellas at The Foster Glass Works, Port Colborne, Ontario, c. 1895.*

In the centre is a free-blown, green glass witch's ball. Circumference 8¾". Burlington Glass Works, Hamilton, Ontario, c. 1905.

Below are two free-blown sock darners. The one on the left is made from amber glass. Length 4⅜". Hamilton Glass Works, Hamilton, Ontario, c. 1890. The darner on the right is in dark amber. Length 4¼". The Foster Glass Works, Port Colborne, Ontario, c. 1897.

FIGURE 35 *Glass hat whimseys were made to hold matches or toothpicks.*

The example on the left was made from a pressed-glass tumbler. Burlington Glass Works, Hamilton, Ontario, c. 1900. The next in line is a top hat made from a pressed glass. The third piece was fashioned from a pressed-glass egg cup; found in clear or opal. Burlington Glass Works, c. 1900.

The item on the far right has the mark of a pontil rod on its base; it was created from a pressed-glass tumbler. Dominion Glass Company, Montreal, P.Q., c. 1920.

FIGURE 36 *A group of glass hat whimseys described below from left to right.*

A glass hat made from a pressed-glass tumbler. Burlington Glass Works, Hamilton, Ontario, c. 1900.

A free-blown hat with a pontil mark on the crown. Montreal, P.Q., c. 1890.

A large, free-blown hat (one of two in the author's collection). This specific design of glass hat is extremely rare, and all examples could be credited to the North American and/or the early Dominion glass companies of Montreal. The rounded crown bears the scar of a pontil rod, the brim has a folded rim, and the crown and rim are joined by a double rim (a technique that could be unique to a specific Canadian glassblower). Length 6⅛". Montreal, c. 1890.

A rare, free-blown hat with the scar of a blow-pipe on the crown. Montreal, c. 1890.

A rare, pressed-glass hat made from a tumbler in the Pillar *design. See* Canadian Glass, *c. 1825-1925, p. 64. The Lamont Glass Company, Trenton, Nova Scotia, c. 1890.*

FIGURE 37 *The pieces shown in this illustration are good examples of the colours encountered by collectors of Canadian glass. They are identified left to right.*

The blown, amber bottle-glass hat has a folded rim and blow-pipe scar on the crown. Width 3⁵/₈". Hamilton Glass Works, Hamilton, Ontario, c. 1870.

The pressed, pale amber cuspidor was made in a one-piece mould. The rayed base is ground and polished. The technique used is seldom encountered and consisted of reheating the upper two-thirds and forming the shoulder, neck and rim. Not a plentiful item. Height, 1³/₄", diameter 2³/₄". Burlington Glass Works, Hamilton, Ontario, c. 1895.

The blue hat was meant as a toothpick holder. Pressed in a two-piece mould. Height 2¹/₄". Burlington Glass Works, c. 1900. The amber hat beside the previous piece is of the same style and size. It was also made at Burlington at about the same time. Both pieces illustrated in Early Canadian Glass, *p. 60.*

The blue glass miniature cuspidor closely resembles the pale amber piece shown second from left. Burlington, c. 1895.

37

FIGURE 38 *Glass cane whimseys. Identified from the lower left to the upper right.*

The piece of a cane in the lower left is an interesting example of a square rod that has been twisted. It illustrates the technique used to enclose four threads of coloured glass in a flint-glass body. Length 12³/8″. Burlington Glass Works, c. 1890.

Above it is a flint-glass cane made square with a twist at the crook. The solid body encases a rod of amber glass. Burlington Glass Works, Hamilton, Ontario, c. 1890.

The solid, flint-glass cane with a twist at the crook and tip was also made at the Burlington Glass Works, c. 1890.

Fourth from the bottom is a very rare "bandmaster's" blown, flint-glass baton with a pale opal-glass swirl throughout the length. Length 40¹/2″. Early Dominion Glass Company, Montreal, P.Q., c. 1886.

Next is a pale aquamarine "twist" glass cane from the Burlington Glass Works, c. 1895.

Sixth from the bottom is a square, flint-glass cane with a twist at the crook and tip. Length 34¹/2″. Diamond Flint Glass, Montreal, c. 1910.

The aquamarine-coloured, bottle-glass cane shown second from the top of the photograph was made in the Humphrey Glass Factory, Trenton, Nova Scotia, c. 1910.

At the top of the illustration is an eight-rod, flint-glass cane with twist at crook and tip. Length 30¹/2″. Burlington Glass Works, c. 1880.

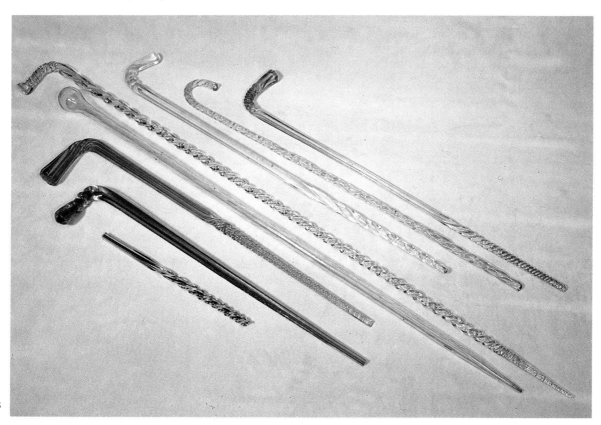

FIGURE 39   *A group of five miniatures. The decanter on the far left (see* Early Canadian Glass *facing p. 61) was a commercial item produced by a technique not too well known to the "new beginner" interested in collecting glass. An examination of the base reveals a swirl terminating in what appears to be a very small pontil mark. We regret to write that this item (and others with a similar mark, like the two examples beside it) was pressed upside down. This allowed the hand-worked plunger to form the fluted neck and the open bottom to be drawn together. Height 3½". Burlington Glass Works, Hamilton, Ontario, c. 1900.*

The pressed, flint-glass "old oaken bucket" with metal bail handle was made in a two-piece mould. Height 1⅞". Burlington Glass Works, Hamilton, Ontario, c. 1900.

The commercial, mould-blown container on the far right has a geometric design, folded rim and rough pontil mark. See Early Canadian Glass, *facing page 61. Height 3⅜". Burlington Glass Works, c. 1875.*

39

FIGURE 40   *A group of four glass-ball whimseys. On the right is a flint-glass witch ball with opal glass "Nailsea" loopings. Circumference 18". Burlington Glass Works, Hamilton, Ontario, c. 1890. In the centre (bottom) is another Burlington witch ball, c. 1890. The mould-blown glass ball in the centre (top) was made in a two-piece mould for use on a lightning rod. Quebec, Ontario, etc., c. 1890. The free-blown, amber witch ball on the left came from the Hamilton Glass Works, Hamilton, Ontario, c. 1895.*

40

FIGURE 41 *Shown here is a rare, off-hand, tricoloured glass drape. The colours are blue, opal and amber. Length of upper chain 45¼", length of link approximately 1¾". See* Canadian Glass c. 1825-1925, *p. 33. Sydenham Glass Company, Wallaceburg, Ontario, c. 1910.*

FIGURE 43 *A pale-aquamarine glass drape with oval links and circular finials. Length 99". Trenton, Nova Scotia, c. 1892.*

FIGURE 42 *This off-hand, multi-coloured drape was made by George Gardiner. The colours include red, white (opal), blue, overlay green, amber and flint glass. Length 72". Burlington Glass Works, Hamilton, Ontario, c. 1890.*

43

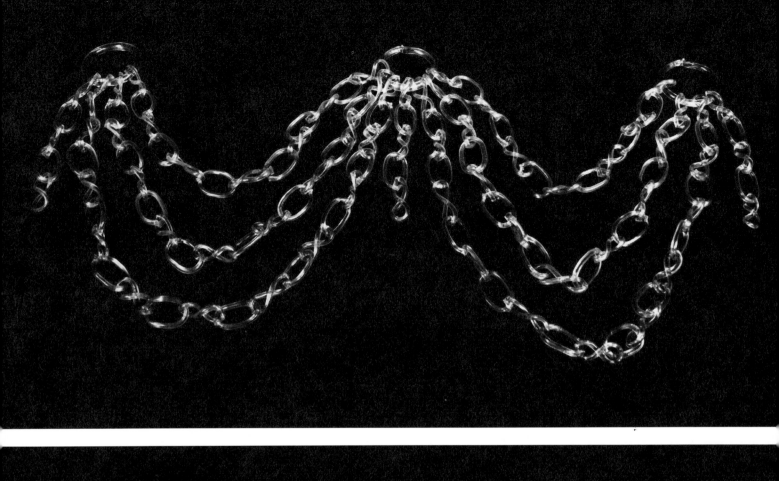

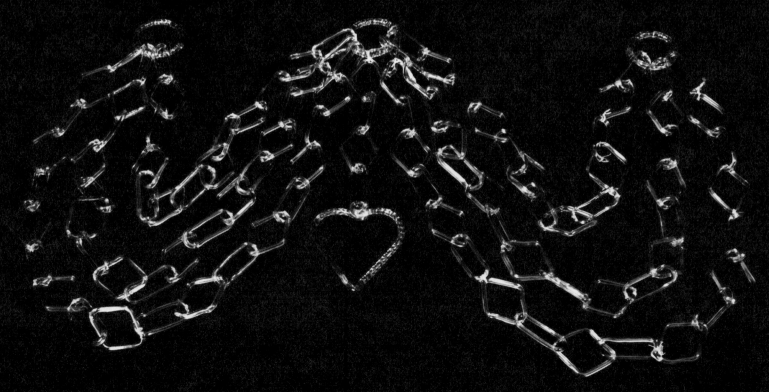

FIGURE 44   *The links are ovoid and "figure-eight" shaped in this flint-glass drape. Length 41¾". See* Early Canadian Glass, *p. 49. Hamilton Glass Works, Hamilton, Ontario, c. 1885.*

FIGURE 45   *A flint-glass drape with one heart-shaped and three circular finials. The links are of diamond and rectangular forms. Length 54". The Diamond Glass Company, Montreal, P.Q., c. 1890.*

FIGURE 46   *A flint-glass drape with triangular and circular finials. The links are of ovoid and figure-eight forms. Length 70". Burlington Glass Works, Hamilton, Ontario c. 1895.*

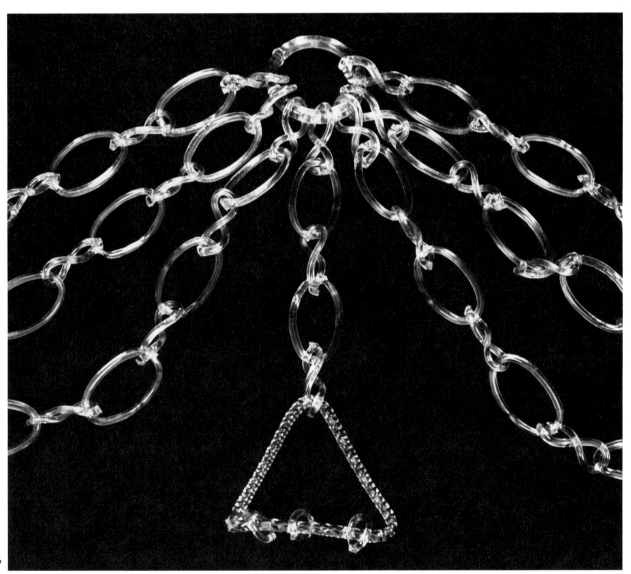

44

46

FIGURE 47 *The rare, flint-glass mud turtle paperweight shown on the left has been included under whimseys, because the technique used in its manufacture is similar to other pieces in this section. One gather of glass was taken, and by use of a spring tool the legs, tail and head were drawn out. Such "turtles" were produced in clear and deep amber bottle glass and presented to school children who were invited to visit the glass factory.*

Foster Bros. Glass Works, Port Colborne, Ontario, c. 1895-1899.

The delicate, tube-glass ship was made at the Sydenham Glass Company, Wallaceburg, Ontario, c. 1920. See Canadian Glass c. 1825-1925, *p. 249.*

47

FIGURE 48 *This baying hound was conceived as part of a land-scape, including hunters, hounds, trees and a hunted deer. The entire scene was meant to be enclosed in a blown-glass dome.*

The hound was blown in the Griner home in Toronto, using opal tube glass, and it dates from the period c. 1898. The finish on this piece suggests the reason for 18th and 19th century dealers and manufacturers using the terms ''pearl,'' ''porcelain,'' ''enamel'' or ''china'' when describing opal glass. The hound measures 5½" in length. See Canadian Glass c. 1825-1925, *p. 250.*

48

THE BURLINGTON GLASS WORKS of Hamilton, Ontario (1876-1909), was the most outstanding, prolific and varied source of late 19th century Canadian lighting equipment designed to burn kerosene. These lamps were interesting, colourful and, in many instances, the mould-blown bowls and pressed-glass bases are found to be a "mix and match" concept in which foot and font might be combined in a series of alternative arrangements of patterns and colours. Comparisons of mixed and matched lamps can provide useful hints for the researcher intent on authenticating new lamps.   G.S.

THE GEORGE GARDINER LAMP

The long search for "The George Gardiner Lamp" had its actual beginnings one winter evening early in 1974 when Gerald and Bea Stevens, my wife, Heidi Redekop, and I were sitting around the dining room table discussing Canadian glass across the remnants of our completed dinner.

A copy of Gerald Stevens' *Canadian Glass c. 1825-1925* lay open at page 227, exposing a full page illustration of the impressive "mould-blown opal glass Burlington Lamp," which Gerald had authenticated as being Burlington.

The evening was progressing as so many evenings did during those winters that the Stevens lived at our home.

Bea could be very mischievous, and Gerald always rose to the bait.

"The shade isn't right," said Bea.

"The shade may be right," responded Gerald. "Compare the colour. Compare the ribbing on the shade and the base of the lamp—they are exactly the same. And the shade is of the period."

Bea pulled the book toward her: "It says here, in Gerald Stevens' book, that 'the shade may or may not be authentic.'"

"That's correct. There are lots of things I believe that I can't prove. I don't have proof."

"The right shade repeats the panel design of the base," insisted Bea. "I know. I saw one when I was a girl."

"That's not proof," said Gerald. "You're reaching back to a memory of maybe fifty years ago. Anyway, Burlington so often mixed and matched. Even if the shade and base were duplicate designs on some, they could be different on others. I should have asked George Gardiner. It's too late for that now."

"I know I'm right," said Bea.

"To prove it we'll have to find one," said Gerald. "And we've never seen one in twenty-five years of collecting."

After twenty-five years of archives and libraries and collections and antique shops and shows, the Stevens had grown a little weary of the endless roads and the unending search for Canadian glass. Gerald and Bea had defined us as their students. They moved into our home for the winter months and every night and every weekend we talked glass, glass, glass. Gerald lectured Heidi and myself on the Canadian glass factories, artisans, products and books that he had studied so long, and the best of which he had written. He assigned us books and cross examined us when they were read. In the field we were now Gerald's eyes and, more importantly, his legs. Occasionally, he and Bea still travelled with us to the shows where he lectured us on the glass and Canadiana offered by the dealers.

"If it's out there we'll find it for you," said Heidi.

It was quickly said but slowly done.

Two years and hundreds of antique shops and shows later we were driving south on Highway 11 to Toronto and swung into *Beryl Bells Antiques*, just north of Richmond Hill.

As we always do, Heidi took one side of the shop, I took the other.

Heidi signalled, and I crossed over.

"It's a discovery and a disappointment in one," she said.

The lamp, electrified, stood on a table, lighting the corner of the shop. The base was clearly the one we sought. But the motif was not repeated in the shade.

I took off the shade, studied it, felt it and handed it to Heidi.

"A copy."

"I'd say a late copy."

"I agree."

The base was right, it was the only one we'd found in two years, and we took it home. Anyway, we had to show it to Gerald and Bea who, in the event, agreed with our conclusion.

More miles. More shops. Finally a repeat of the process in Sherbrooke, in the Eastern Townships of Quebec.

We were visiting our young people on their farm at Glen Sutton, and when they found they had to go to Sherbrooke to shop, I decided to go along. Heidi decided to stay on the farm. And in a Sherbrooke antique shop, the name of which I forget, our lamp was sitting on a table in a back room. Again the shade was a modern copy.

"Bea," I said, later at home, "are you certain that we're not hunting for something that doesn't exist?"

"Just listen to him," responded Bea. "Tired after three years and two bases that are right. In twenty-five years we only found the one that's in the book!"

It was on a sunny Saturday morning in June of 1978 that Bea Stevens phoned and asked us to come up to spend the day with them at their summer place at Oro Station on Lake Simcoe, north of Barrie. We packed a box with pieces of glass that we had found since we last saw them. We did this with every piece of glass that we found: it allowed Gerald to authenticate it, to consider it for inclusion in the collector's book on glass he was already considering and, using the new pieces as examples, to continue to advance our education in Canadian glass.

After lunch Gerald and Bea and Heidi were engaged in various activities.

"I think I'll just run across to Bill Cole's shop and see if he has any new lamps," I said.

"Don't get visiting so many shops that you're late for dinner," said Bea.

In fact, I was back in less than half an hour.

Bill's truck was in his driveway, so I knew he was home. Bill operates a "by chance or appointment" shop. He came to the door when I knocked.

What Bill has he may or may not sell. He is a real authority on carnival glass, and it competes for his regard with coal-oil lamps. I had acquired lamps from Bill from time to time, but generally it was a matter of making a swap. Some things he wouldn't part with at all.

Bill threw the light switch in his glass-filled basement room and, facing me, sitting on the floor, was the base of our Burlington lamp.

Beside it sat the shade—the right shade—Bea Stevens' shade—the shade that duplicated the motif of the base—the shade that had evaded us all for so many years.

I looked at some other lamps, some other glass, and finally picked up the lamp I wanted, then the shade.

They were positively right!

"Will you sell this, Bill?" I asked.

"Sure. You saw the hairline cracks in the shade?"

"Yes."

"How about thirty-five dollars?"

"Very reasonable."

"I work on a percentage. I bought that cheap with a bunch of things at a farm auction. Thirty-five is just fine."

I couldn't get back to the Stevens' place fast enough. I unwrapped the lamp and put it on a table in the porch, then called Gerald and Bea and Heidi.

"I said so!" said Bea. "I knew it! I told you so!"

"At last!" said Heidi. "Good for you!"

"The proof!" said Gerald. "You were right, Bea, and now we have the ultimate proof—the piece itself! It isn't a theory or a memory any more. Now we have the beautiful proof!"

Gerald took off the shade and turned it over in his hands. "I think I would like to name this in honour of George Gardiner. He was a fine glassworker and, through him, I learned a lot about how things were made and the things that were made at Burlington and other glass factories. He may even have made this lamp. Let's name this pattern "The George Gardiner Lamp."

"I like that," said Bea.

Gerald had taken up the base and was studying the painting on it. "It would be interesting to find out who did the painting of the lamps for the Burlington Glass Works," he said. "Studying the techniques of the painters on known Burlington lamps might be a useful means of identification. If another lamp was painted in a similar design or manner, it would be indicative, at least, that it was Burlington."

Heidi and I thought of that five year search, now completed.

Neither of us said a word.   R.H.

49

50

FIGURE 49 *The original Gardiner Lamp published on page 227 of* Canadian Glass c. 1825-1925. *Mould-blown, opal glass. Height of base 6/4"; diameter 6". Is the shade an original, a "mix and match?" Perhaps. The ribbed motif repeats the base, the colours match, the shade is of the period. But Bea Stevens always argued the shade should exactly duplicate the base. The shade is 5⅛" in height, 8" in diameter. The lamp is authenticated by many Burlington shards. With the Hedlins, we searched for a lamp in which the base design was repeated in the shade.*

FIGURE 50 *In the years that followed, the Hedlins found the two others shown here . . . the bases were right, the shades were not original. But Bea Stevens still insisted that out there, somewhere, was a lamp with a shade of the same design.*

FIGURE 51 *Bea was right. On a sunny, summer Saturday Ralph Hedlin dropped in at Bill Cole's shop at Oro Station, just north of Barrie, Ontario. And there was the lamp base and, beside it, the shade that duplicated the design and painting of the base. We had the ultimate proof—the piece itself—the George Gardiner Lamp of Burlington.*

FIGURE 52 *On the left is a mould-blown, flint-glass lamp bowl decorated with a* Daisy and Button *design. The base is of pressed glass, and the foot is decorated in a* Rain Drop *pattern with a serrated edge. Height 6³/4".*

Beside it is a pressed, flint-glass salver with the same Rain Drop *design seen in the foot of the lamp on the left. Height 5¹/4"; diameter 9". Burlington Glass Works, Hamilton, Ontario, c. 1890.*

52

FIGURE 53 *On the left is a mould-blown, flint-glass hand lamp decorated with the* Bead and Petal *motif: the handle is pressed flint-glass. Height 3¹/8".*

The same motif is used in the flint-glass, footed lamp (centre) which has a bowl and foot blown in a three-piece mould. Height 9¹/4".

Bead and Petal *also decorates the flint-glass hand lamp on the right. Mould-blown bowl with pressed-glass base. The base has a "Petal" motif, and the foot and handle are of one piece. Height 5¹/8". Burlington Glass Works.*

53

FIGURE 54 *This deep amber coloured lamp has a mould-blown bowl and pressed-glass base decorated with a* Daisy and Button *motif.*

This specific form of bowl is to be found in a variety of sizes and colours, including clear flint, pale and deep amber, cranberry and opal, flint and opal, etc.

The upper rim of the flint-glass chimney illustrates the ''Burlington crimp,'' numerous shards of which were obtained while excavating this specific site which is now honoured by an Historic Sites plaque.

This chimney was given special attention and was sand-blasted to obtain a lightly opaque area which is wheel-engraved with floral chips. See Early Canadian Glass, *p. 62.*

Height (less chimney) 9½".

54

FIGURE 55 *On the far left and second from the right is a very rare pair of lamps with bowls bearing forms of* Cross *and* Coin Dot *motifs in opal glass. These bowls illustrate the variants which were created in the Burlington Glass Works factory. Both have flint-glass,* Chevron *bases. Height (less chimneys) 7³⁄₈".*

The two finger lamps are decorated with the Coin Dot *motif. Both were mould-blown in a two-piece mould and have applied handles. The piece on the right is made of blue and white opal glass, and the other light amber and white opal. Height (less chimneys) 3".*

55

FIGURE 56 *On the left is a mould-blown, flint-glass lamp bowl with pressed flint-glass base. A similar piece was illustrated and named* Buttons and Bows *in George MacLaren's* Nova Scotia Glass, *page 40. Height 8¼".*

In the centre is a lamp with a base identical to the preceding piece. The mould-blown, hand-painted font is decorated with a landscape and farmhouse scene on a frosted-glass background. Height (less chimney) 8¾".

On the right is a lamp with a mould-blown, flint-glass bowl and two-piece, mould-pressed base. Although the base is identical to that shown in MacLaren, the bowl differs in form. In Nova Scotia, as elsewhere in Canada, different lamp bowls and different fonts were "mixed and matched."

56

FIGURE 57 *The lamp on the left has a pressed, flint-glass base and* Frame and Sprig *bowl. Height (less chimney) 8³/8".*

Four Frame and Sprig *motifs decorate the mould-blown bowl of the lamp in the centre. The pressed-glass base is of a design which may be found associated with various designs of ''mix and match'' bowl. Height (less chimney) 9¹/4".*

The flint-glass bowl on the right was mould-blown in a three-piece mould. It is decorated with a Squirrel and Tree *motif. The base of this rare piece was pressed in a two-piece mould. Height (less chimney) 6³/4". Burlington Glass Works.*

FIGURE 58 *The footed finger lamp on the left is decorated in the* Coin Dot *motif. Blown in a two-piece mould with applied handle attached to base and font. Clear glass and white opal dots with ''mix and match'' base. Height (less chimney) 4³/4".*

In the centre is a light blue lamp with two-piece, mould-blown bowl and pressed, Chevron *base. Height (less chimney) 9".*

On the right is a honey amber, footed hand lamp with a Wheel *font and* Chevron *foot. Font blown in a two-piece mould. Foot pressed in a three-piece mould. Handle pressed in a two-piece mould. Many of this design of handle excavated at the Burlington site. Height (less chimney) 4⁷/8".*

58

FIGURE 59   *Three examples with mould-blown, flint-glass bowls and pressed glass bases all with the* Bull's-Eye *motif. See* Canadian Glass, *c. 1825-1925, facing p. 21.*

   The base of the left-hand example is made of white opal. Height (less chimney) 8³/8". The deep green base of the centre lamp is not common. Height (less chimney) 8³/8". The base of the piece on the right is in blue opal glass. Height (less chimney) 10³/4".

59

FIGURE 60 *Two lamps with decorated bases. On the left is an example with a mould-blown, flint-glass bowl featuring a* Leaf and Dart *motif. The base is of pressed flint glass. Height (less chimney) 8³/4".*

The very interesting flint-glass lamp on the right has a bowl blown in a three-piece mould and decorated with butterfly, floral, horseshoe and anchor motifs. The pressed-glass base has a column and four Fan *motifs on an octagonal foot. Height (less chimney) 9¹/8". Burlington Glass Works, Hamilton, Ontario, c. 1885.*

FIGURE 61 *This two-piece, mould-blown hand lamp has a rayed base and applied handle. Burlington Glass Works, Hamilton, Ontario (and elsewhere), c. 1890.*

60

61

FIGURE 62 *The font of this library lamp features an etched beaver motif. Burlington Glass Works, Hamilton, Ontario, c. 1890.*

62

FIGURE 63 *A group of deep green coloured Bull's-Eye lamps. The bowls have been blown in a three-piece mould, while the bases have been pressed in a four-piece mould. When the collars are removed, the roughness of the blow-pipe scars may be seen. Height (left to right, less chimneys) 8", 4³/₄" and 2³/₄".*

63

FIGURE 64 *Four hand lamps from the Bur-lington Glass Works, Hamilton, Ontario.*

On the far left and second from right is a pair in deep and medium amber respectively. Both have applied handles and Rayed *bases. Height (less chimneys) 3¹/₈". Circa 1880.*

Second from left is a mould-blown, green-glass, "nutmeg" hand lamp with wire han-dle. Height 2¹/₁₆". Circa 1890.

On the far right is a rare, amber, mould-blown hand lamp with Diamond *quilted de-sign, applied handle and* Wheel *motif on the base. Height (less chimney) 3". Circa 1875.*

FIGURE 65 *All four lamps illustrated here were blown from opal glass. The mould-blown "nutmeg" hand lamp on the left has a brass wire handle; it was made in a two-piece mould. Height (less chimney) 2¹/₁₆". Burlington Glass Works, Hamilton, Ontario, c. 1890.*

Second from left is a similar mould-blown "nutmeg" lamp with wire handle and opal, *ball shade. Height 2¹/₈"; overall height 6¹/₂". Burlington Glass Works, c. 1890.*

The mould-blown hand lamp third from the left is decorated with a filigree motif. Made in a two-piece mould. Height 2¹/₄", diameter 3".

The rare, free-blown hand lamp on the right has an applied handle. Height 2³/₈". Burlington Glass Works, c. 1880.

65

FIGURE 66 *All three of these lamps were made in the Burlington Glass Works, Hamilton, Ontario, circa 1890.*

The piece on the left has a mould-blown bowl with a Wheel *motif. Brass collar, flint-glass column and bronzed, cast-iron base. The mould-blown column had been decorated with an interior floral design of coloured paper. Height (less chimney) 10¾″.*

The flint-glass, footed lamp in the centre has a mould-blown bowl with miniature Wheel *motifs. Blown in a three-piece mould. The mould-blown foot is decorated with vestiges of a ''Flowers in Basket'' printed design. Two-piece mould; brass collars; cast-iron base. Height (less chimney) 11¾″.*

On the right is a flint-glass, footed lamp. The mould-blown bowl is decorated with a Fan and Diamond *motif. The mould-blown, flint-glass column has inner decoration.*

66

FIGURE 67 *On the left is a mould-blown, footed lamp in dark amber.* Chevron *base. Height (less chimney) 8".*

The mould-blown bowl of the piece in the centre is in amber glass with a Cross *design. Pressed, flint,* Chevron *base. Height (less chimney) 8".*

The dark amber lamp on the right has a two-piece, mould-blown bowl and pressed, Chevron *base. Height (less chimney) 6¾".*

FIGURE 68 *Two "L'Ange Gardien, Extra. C. H. Binks & Co. Montreal" hand lamps blown in two-piece moulds and with applied handles.*

The example on the left has a blue base and globular ball shade. Height 3¹/₈". Although produced for nineteenth century Quebec, shards confirm these beautiful little lamps were made at the Burlington Glass Works, Hamilton, Ontario, c. 1880.

The piece on the right has an amber font and swirled, globular ball shade in ruby. Height 3¹/₈". Burlington Glass Works, c. 1880.

Similar lamps without the legend imprinted on the font are not *Canadian. The unsigned lamps were made in France and shipped to distributors in Montreal in large quantities during this century. As late as the 1950s I personally examined, in a Montreal warehouse, boxes of such unsigned lamps, shipped from France, similar to the early, authentic, Canadian-made lamps with the embossed Binks legend. The unsigned lamps were still to be found for sale in Montreal retail establishments in the early 1960s.*

FIGURE 69 *Both lamps in this illustration have bowls blown in a two-piece mould and decorated with the* Sawtooth *design.*

The smaller of the two is made of clear glass on a white opal base. Height (less chimney) 9³/₄".

The larger example has a flint and opal foot. A brass collar joins the flint bowl to the opal, one-piece column and base which was pressed in a three-piece mould. Height (less chimney) 14". Burlington Glass Works, Hamilton, Ontario, c. 1875.

FIGURE 70 *On the left is a lamp with a mould-blown, flint-glass bowl decorated in the* Panel *design. Pressed flint-glass base with eight fleurs-de-lis. Height (less chimney) 8⁵/₈". Made in Burlington and Montreal, c. 1890-1900.*

On the right is a flint-glass lamp with an undecorated, two-piece, mould-blown bowl. It is a variant and was given a base which is similar to those associated with Frame and Sprig *lamps. Height (less chimney) 7⁷/₈".*

69

70

FIGURE 71 *The* Fish-Scale *design decorates the mould-blown bowl and flint-glass base of the lamp on the left. Height (less chimney) 5⅝".*

On the right is a flint-glass, footed lamp. Bowl mould-blown in a three-piece mould decorated with the Canadian Cable *motif. Base pressed in a two-piece mould with* Drop *and* Picket *designs. Height (less chimney) 9". Burlington Glass Works, Hamilton, Ontario, c. 1895.*

FIGURE 72 *A pair of lamps with mould-blown bowls decorated with the* Daisy *and* Button *motif. The feet are of moulded brass, the bases of cast-iron. Height (less chimneys) 7".*

71

72

FIGURE 73 *This lamp was made with a two-part, mould-blown, opal glass base and shade. Cast-iron foot and cast-brass collars. The upper area of the shade has a circle of* Fleur-de-Lis *motifs. The decorations have been painted and fired. Only specimens known to the author. Shards. Height 17"; diameter of shade 9¼". Burlington Glass Works, Hamilton, Ontario, c. 1890.*

73

FIGURE 74 *A three-part, mould-blown, opal glass, footed lamp. Cast-iron base and brass fittings. The painted floral motifs on this very rare lamp are all original. Only example known to the author. I would appreciate information regarding any other specimens. Shards. Height 20⅛". Burlington Glass Works, Hamilton, Ontario, c. 1890.*

FIGURE 75 *The two lamps on the left are decorated with the* 101 *design. The piece on the far left has a mould-blown, flint-glass bowl,* Rayed *base and applied handle. Made in a two-piece mould. Height 3". The piece next to it has a pressed-glass base with the* Colonial *motif. Height 7¹/₂".*

The two pieces on the right are discussed in Early Canadian Glass, *pages 108 and 62, respectively. The flint-glass hand lamp next to the footed* 101 *lamp was mould-blown with a ribbed design; applied handle and* Rayed *base. Height 3". Attributed to the glass houses of Vaudreuil, presumably The Canada Glass Company, Hudson, P.Q., c. 1865-1875, and the other (p. 62) to the Burlington Glass Works, Hamilton, Ontario, c. 1870-1900. The mould-blown, flint-glass hand lamp on the far right has a ribbed design,* Rayed *base and applied handle. Burlington Glass Works, c. 1875.*

75

FIGURE 76 *On the far left is a mould-blown, flint-glass, ''Little Buttercup'' hand lamp. Applied, trailed handle. Height 2³⁄₈''. Burlington Glass Works, Hamilton, Ontario, c. 1890.*

Second from left is a bilingual ''L'Ange Gardien—C. H. Binks & Co.'' blown, two-mould, flint-glass hand lamp with applied handle. Height (less chimney) 2¹⁄₈''. Burlington Glass Works, c. 1880.

In the centre is a mould-blown ''Little Banner'' flint-glass lamp. Height 1¹⁄₈''. Diamond Flint Glass, Montreal, P.Q., and elsewhere, c. 1905.

Second from right is another example of the type of piece shown second from left. Height 2¹⁄₈''. Burlington Glass Works, c. 1880.

On the far right is a mould-blown, footed, ''Improved Banner'' flint-glass lamp. Height 3⁵⁄₈''. Montreal and elsewhere, c. 1905.

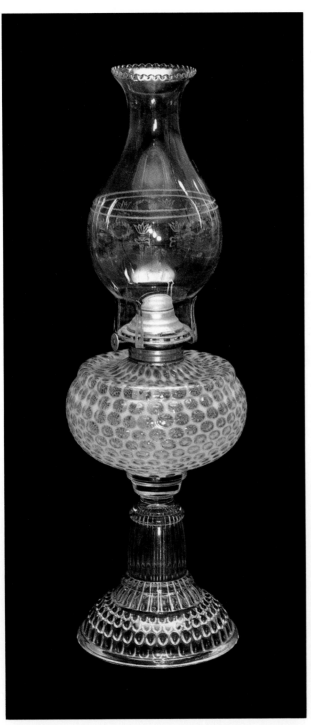

77

FIGURE 77 *This lamp, with its blue bowl and clear base, is the same as the rare example shown in Figure 85, but this example is in the blue glass made at Burlington.*

FIGURE 78 *Three lamps with bowls decorated in the* Thousand Eye *pattern.*

On the left, the bowl is of mould-blown blue glass. Brass collars. Mould-blown, opal glass column with painted floral motifs. Cast-iron base. Burlington Glass Works, Hamilton, Ontario, c. 1885.

In the centre, the bowl is of mould-blown amber glass decorated with Button and Band *motifs. Height (less chimney) 8". Burlington Glass Works, c. 1885.*

On the right, the bowl is of mould-blown clear glass. The clear glass column has also been mould-blown and decorated with a Button and Band *base. Height (less chimney) 9$^{1}/_{2}$".*

FIGURE 79 *On the left is a lamp with a mould-blown bowl made of light amber glass in the upper portion and frosted glass below. Pressed, flint-glass* Waterfall *base. Height (less chimney) 7".*

The example in the centre has a two-piece, mould-blown, flint-glass bowl with a pressed glass Chevron *base. Height (less chimney) 8¼".*

On the right is a lamp with a mould-blown, five-piece bowl decorated in the Cross *design;* Chevron *base; flint glass. Height (less chimney) 8⅛".*

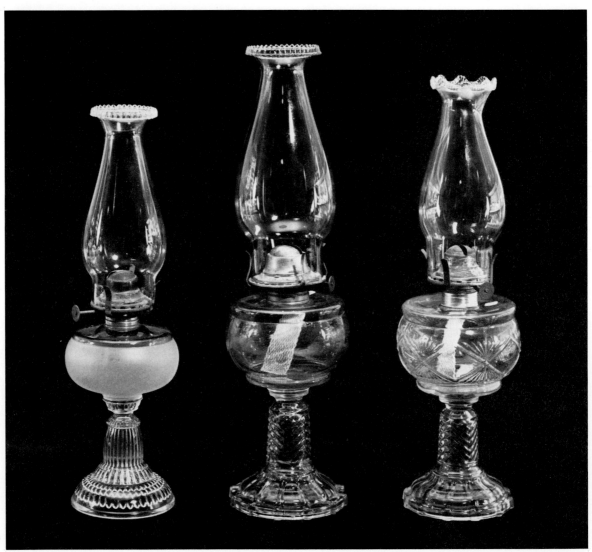

79

FIGURE 80 *In the foreground of this illustration is a flint-glass hand lamp blown in a two-piece mould and decorated with the* Wheel *motif. The handle is applied pressed glass. Height (less chimney) 2⁷⁄₈".*

The three lamps in the background are all related. In the centre is a blown, flint, footed lamp with blue-opal column. The Wheel *motif that it shares with the other pieces shown here has proven to be most interesting in the study of early Canadian glass and has assisted in*

identifying additional specimens. This example combines brass, iron, opal and flint glass. The iron base has been painted with bronze. Height (less chimney) 11⁷⁄₈".

The piece on the far left has an identical font with a variation in the column and foot.

On the far right is a similar lamp with a white opal column and cast-iron base. A "mix and match" lamp very typical of the Burlington Glass Works, Hamilton, Ontario.

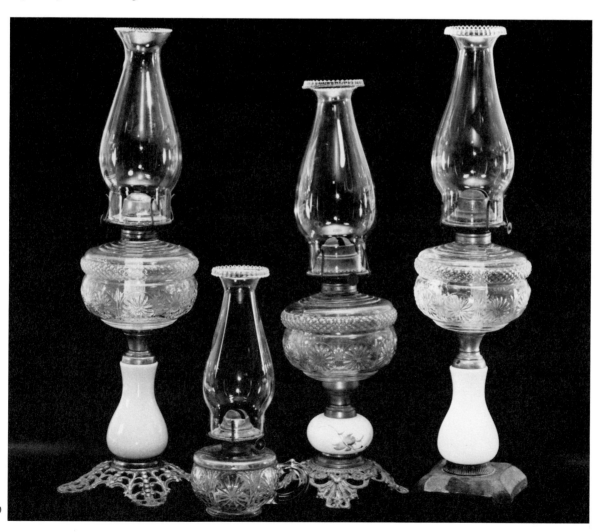

80

FIGURE 81 *The lamp on the left was made with a light amber, two-piece, mould-blown bowl and pressed, clear* Chevron *base. The bowl is an interesting variant and illustrates what we classify as a* Wheel *motif. Height (less chimney) 7³/4″.*

The mould-blown amber bowl of the centre piece is decorated with a Cross *motif. Pressed, flint-glass base; foot in* Chevron *design; and base in* Cross *motif. Height (less chimney) 8¹/4″. Burlington Glass Works, Hamilton, Ontario, c. 1890.*

On the right is a lamp with a mould-blown, dark amber bowl decorated with a Cross *design. The shape of this bowl corresponds with that of the lamp on the far left. Pressed, flint-glass base with* Chevron *pattern. Height (less chimney) 9³/4″.*

FIGURE 82 *The smaller of the two lamps in this photograph has a mould-blown font with swirled stripes of diagonal white opal over clear, diagonal bands. Clear glass foot and base with* Chevron *design. Two-piece mould. Height (less chimney) 7¹/₂".*

The larger lamp illustrates a mould-blown font in honey amber decorated with swirled strips of white opal. The pressed-glass base is of a similar colour and, to the collector who is doing personal research relative to early Canadian glass lamps, is of a specific design which has been classified as Chevron. *This design is to be found associated with numerous bowls of varied form. Height (less chimney) 9⁵/₈". Burlington Glass Works, Hamilton, Ontario, c. 1880.*

FIGURE 83 *All three examples in this illustration have mould-blown, flint-glass bowls with the* Panel *design. The piece on the left has a pressed-glass handle; height 4⅛". The lamp in the centre features a pressed-glass handle and a base having* Ray *and* Diamond *motifs; height (less chimney) 4⅛". The pressed-glass base of the lamp on the right is a variant of the* Ray *and* Diamond *design; height 7".*

83

FIGURE 84 *The lamp on the left has a mould-blown two piece bowl; three-piece, pressed* Chevron *post; and a one-piece, pressed* Cross *foot. All in flint glass. Height 7".*

The piece second from left has a mould-blown, five-piece bowl with Cross *design; three-piece, pressed* Chevron *post; and one-piece, applied, pressed foot with* Cross *motif. Height (less chimney) 7½".*

The example second from right has a mould-blown, flint-glass, two-piece bowl similar to that shown in Figure 87; and a flint-glass base decorated with a geometric "Daisy." Height 7".

The lamp on the far right has a mould-blown, five-piece bowl with Cross *design; and a* Chevron *base. Both in flint glass. Height 6½".*

FIGURE 85 *Three lamps decorated with the* Honeycomb *design in flint and opal glass. The hand lamp on the left has a pressed, flint-glass base with a* Block *motif. Height (less chimney) 4¼". The pressed flint-glass bases on the remaining two pieces are decorated with a* Waterfall *pattern. The lamp on the far right (height, less chimney, 8½") is a particularly rare form.*

85

FIGURE 86 *Mould-blown bowls with cranberry and white opal* Honeycomb *designs, as well as flint-glass bases decorated with* Waterfall *motifs, characterize these two lamps. The hand lamp has an applied handle. Authenticated Canadian lamps in cranberry are rare. This lamp is also shown in blue and white opal. Height (less chimney) 4¹/₄″. The footed lamp measures 7³/₄″ high (less chimney).*

FIGURE 87 *The mould-blown flint-glass bowl of the lamp on the left is decorated with the* Daisy and Button *motif. Pressed-glass base with plain, circular column and square foot decorated with a variant geometric* Daisy *motif. Height (less chimney) 8½".*

The mould-blown bowl of the piece in the centre is of the same form as that shown in Figure 84. The pressed-glass base is from a three-piece mould having a foot decorated with a Rain Drop *design terminating in a serrated edge. Height 8³/₈".*

On the right is a flint-glass lamp with a mould-blown bowl and pressed base, both of which are decorated with the Daisy and Button *motif. This bowl is found in a variety of sizes with pressed-glass bases of several designs. Height 9⁵/₈".*

87

FIGURE 88 *On the left is a flint-glass lamp with a mould-blown bowl in the* Palmette *motif. The design of the pressed base is worthy of attention, because it is useful in authenticating additional Canadian glass lamps. Height 8⅞".*

The flint-glass lamp with the plain, mould-blown bowl is identifiable as being an example of early Canadian glass by the specific form of the base. Compare this example with the previous piece. Height (less chimney) 8¾".

Another example with a similar base is shown on the far right. The specific design on the mould-blown, flint-glass bowl is to be found decorating pressed glass, tableware, etc. Height 8".

Please note that the pressed bases in all these examples are duplicates.

FIGURE 89 *This lamp, authenticated by shards found at the site of the Burlington Glass Works, is the only example known to the author—it may be unique. The author would be very pleased to be advised of any other examples known. It is two-part mould blown. The foot is cast-iron, the collar cast-brass. The upper area of the shade has a circle of* fleurs-de-lis; *the decoration is painted and fired. A very important and rare—perhaps unique—Burlington lamp. Overall height 17"; diameter of the shade 9³/4". Circa 1890.*

89

FIGURE 90 *This mould-blown, blue-glass nutmeg hand lamp with wire handle was made at the Burlington Glass Works, Hamilton, Ontario, c. 1890. Height (less chimney) 2¹/₁₆".*

FIGURE 91 *On the left is very beautiful, mould-blown, blue-opal lamp with a beaded* Fern *motif. Made in a four-piece mould. Height 2¹/₄"; diameter 2⁵/₈".* See Canadian Glass, c. 1825-1925, *p. 219. Authenticated by shards found at the site of the Burlington Glass Works. Circa 1890.*

The similar piece on the right bears the same motif, as well as its original enamelled decoration. Four-piece mould. Height 2¹/₄", diameter 2⁵/₈". Burlington Glass Works, Hamilton, Ontario, c. 1890.

90

91

FIGURE 92 *Each of the bases shown here is decorated with the* Canadian Drape *motif. The miniature-footed, flint-glass lamp on the left measures 6½" high (less chimney). The flint-glass bowl of the example in the centre was blown in a two-piece mould. Pressed, flint-glass base. The foot is octagonal and rests on eight scalloped feet; height (less chimney) is 11¾"; made at the Burlington Glass Works,* Hamilton, Ontario, c. 1875. On the right is a similar example; height 11¾".*

The two larger lamps have been shown here to illustrate the complete Drape *motif.*

92

FIGURE 93 *Three lamps with* Bull's-Eye *designs and white opal bases. All have mould-blown, flint-glass bowls and pressed bases. The piece on the left measures 10⅝″ high (less chimney).*

The footed hand lamp on the right is a somewhat rare form, and it illustrates an interesting technique. The base and handle were pressed in a four-piece mould having one wall of a greater thickness and of a height that would accomodate the molten glass forming the handle. When taken from the mould, the handle would be reheated, bent and inserted into the bowl. Height 5¼″.

93

FIGURE 94 *On the left is a green glass, footed lamp. The bowl was mould-blown in a three-piece mould and decorated with the* Canadian Cable *motif. The base was pressed in a two-piece mould and decorated with* Drop and Picket *motifs. Height (less chimney) 9⁷/₈". Burlington Glass Works, Hamilton, Ontario, c. 1895.*

In the centre is a flint-glass, footed lamp in machine-made amber glass. Fluted foot and bowl made in one piece. Although common in clear glass, this lamp is rarely found in amber. See Canadian Glass, c. 1825-1925, *p. 130. Height (less chimney) 7³/₄".*

The lamp on the right has a mould-blown, green glass bowl with Leaf and Fan *motif. Pressed, green glass base with* Fan *design. See* Canadian Glass, c. 1825-1925, *p. 16. Height (less chimney) 7¹/₂".*

94

FIGURE 95 *A selection of deep green* Bull's-Eye *lamps. Heights (less chimneys) left to right: 10³/4", 10", 9¹/2", 8¹/2".*

95

96

FIGURE 96 *The lamp on the left of the illustration is an interesting example of a series of lamps which are found in a variety of forms. The basic similarity is represented by the mould-blown glass fonts decorated with various motifs, including the well known* Daisy and Button *pattern. The column is of mould-blown opal glass decorated with a painted pansy and foliage motifs. The collars are of moulded brass, and the foot is of cast-iron. Height (less chimney) 12³/8". Burlington Glass Works, Hamilton, Ontario, c. 1885.*

On the right is a variant with a pale blue font. Height (less chimney) 11¹/4".

FIGURE 97 *The clues provided by the Canadian lamp on the far right allow authentication of the example on the far left. The left-hand lamp, in turn, provides additional data relative to mould-blown Canadian glass bowls. The bowl is of pale amber glass and is decorated with several designs, including the* Block *motif which was quite popular with Canadian glass manufacturers. Height (less chimney) 12¹/8".*

The piece on the right has a mould-blown font with a Wheel *motif. Height (less chimney) 12¹/2".*

The bases on all three lamps are of a most interesting design; they supply additional data relative to early Canadian lighting. Burlington Glass Works, Hamilton, Ontario, c. 1890.

5 NEW PATTERNS OF CANADIAN PRESSED GLASS

MY PRINCIPAL INTEREST has always been the researching of the early Canadian glass factories, interviewing those who worked in them and through this and other means, authenticating Canadian glass in all its many forms. I have initiated or taken part in many excavations of glass factory sites—a very different kind of research—finding information with respect to the factories and seeking shards that enable the researcher to authenticate patterns of pressed tableware or other Canadian glass factory products.

Shards from the old site, if very professionally collected and authenticated as being from the production areas, provide a means of establishing irrefutably that a particular pattern was made in that factory.

For the researcher, the authentication as Canadian of a pattern is an exhilarating event—one which I have experienced many times. In addition to identifying patterns in this section that I have not previously been able to prove, of my own knowledge, were Canadian, I wish to try and share some of the excitement that attends matching a shard from one of the old factories to a piece of pressed glass on an antique dealer's shelf.

I should explain that a "shard" is a portion of glass from a broken goblet, plate or anything made at a factory and, to be relevant, excavated on the factory site. To be useful for purposes of authentication it must be distinctive enough in pattern or other characteristics to permit the researcher-collector to confirm that it came from a specific piece of patterned glass.

I have a box of shards, excavated on the Burlington site. Bea Stevens and I have been working for years attempting to authenticate patterns from these shards. The procedure is to carry the shards and, through visiting shows, shops or any other place where old glass can be found and examined, to try and match the shard to a complete piece.

The physical demands became too much for us and Ralph Hedlin and Heidi Redekop—our friends and my students in glass—undertook to continue the search.

Armed with the shards they took up the hunt. The arrangement was that they would buy any pattern that seemed to match a shard. They would bring shard and the glass article to me. I would do the final authentication.

Over a period of years of search and after thousands of miles of driving and hundreds of shops and shows, they have helped us to reduce the number of unproven shards in the box by ten—eight patterns of tableware and two individual table pieces—a bread plate and a small fish dish. These ten patterns I was able to positively authenticate as having been made in the Burlington Glass Works in Hamilton.

Our first great success was with the pattern that I have called *Button and Buckle*. The four of us had driven north of Toronto. We had been invited to call for a cup of tea with Lena Stanbury in Stouffville. Lena was one of the great glass dealers.

Perhaps because of our great interest in glass, Lena Stanbury used on her tea table a very handsome setting of a pattern we had always taken to be only an American one called *Thousand Eye Three Panel.*

We were driving away when something clicked in my mind.

"Just stop a minute, will you," I said.

I reached for the box of shards and found the piece that was nagging at me.

"Let's go back," I said.

I laid the shard against Lena's creamer. It was perfect. The pattern was made in Burlington!

We subsequently saw many pieces and, interestingly enough, most were light or dark amber. On a happy day the Hedlin's found a bowl in the same pattern in perfect Burlington blue in Short's Antiques in Newcastle. Burlington had produced the pattern in clear glass and in the three colored glasses so frequently used in that factory—dark amber, light amber and blue.

I have always been opposed to adopting American names for patterns that were made in Canadian factories. I named this pattern *Button and Buckle*.

Over the years that followed there was much digging in the shard box and much studying. Other patterns were proven. There are two discoveries that I still find exciting when I think of them.

It was the middle of the week, Bea and I were at the Hedlins, Ralph was at work and Heidi, with the box of shards, was scouting the Toronto antique shops in the continuing search for new glass patterns.

She came home in the late afternoon.

"I've found something very interesting and very beautiful in a shop on Bayview Avenue," she said. "Will you come and look at it?"

In the back of the shop she pointed to a shelf.

"Just quietly buy it," I said.

"All of it?"

"Yes".

Back in the car, the glass wrapped and with us, I said, "Heidi, you've made an unbelievably important find."

Ralph was home when we got there. We unwrapped the pieces. Included was a complete table setting—creamer, spooner, butter dish and sugar—a covered comport and a water jug. It was a variant of a *Daisy and Button* pattern, the creamer and jug had hand-applied handles, all parts that had no pattern were acid-etched, and beautiful designs were cut on every piece. It was a clear, bright flint glass—one of the truly beautiful things Burlington had produced.

"I consider this pattern to be uniquely Canadian," I said. "It is positively Burlington. The last time I saw the pattern was in George Gardiner's home. He had a creamer, and he told me they made this pattern and design at Burlington when he was a glassblower there. I have seen the shards when we were excavating at Burlington. It is pressed, then acid-etched, then cut. In each piece there are examples of three different glass decoration techniques. It is an important find."

Bea and I agreed that, in honour of the person who found it, we would call this the *Heidi* pattern.

I cannot consider every pattern but some are more interesting than others, and I will record the authentication of one pattern that illustrates how sheer persistence can finally pay off.

Authenticating with shards is much more difficult than it sounds. With many shards, particularly if the pattern is not strongly marked and differentiated, you must find a piece of tableware identical to the one from which the shard originally came. If the piece with which you are comparing is a shard from a goblet, for example, and you are looking at a jug that, in fact, is of the right pattern you are more likely to miss it than not because the shard doesn't obviously fit the larger statement of the pattern. So you might try it on a series of pieces that are right, but unless you measured it against the goblet, you might well miss it.

One day Ralph decided that he would take a single shard and for six months attempt only to find the pattern to which it belonged. The shard he chose was a small piece, double the size of a man's thumbnail, covered in a uniform variation of a tree of life pattern.

"I'm going to find where this belongs," he told us.

It was a particularly difficult piece because the pattern was so much the same across the whole shard, but that was the one he chose. The shard was broken from the edge—one side was polished —and it was slightly scalloped.

"My judgment is that I am looking for a glass bowl," said Ralph. "A wavy edge wouldn't be on a goblet, I don't think it would look good on a creamer or jug."

"That's a very plain pattern, and if it is from a bowl I'd think the same pattern is probably uniform over the whole bowl," said Heidi.

"It would be ugly that way so there must be something to keep it from being ugly," said Bea.

In the event it proved to be a reasonably good collective analysis. But the pattern wouldn't let itself be discovered. Ralph and Heidi brought everything home that had that kind of a solid, tree of life pattern but, twist and turn the shard and compare as we would, it just wouldn't work. Several times we failed.

Another day Ralph had been in Ottawa on business and Heidi had waited dinner. When he came in he went over and cleared a spot and set a brown paper bag in the middle of the dining room table.

"I had an hour before my plane and went into a shop. Do you want to eat or see what I found?"

Ralph was clearly pleased with himself.

"I want to see what it is," said Heidi. "Gerald, why don't you do the honours."

When I held it in my hand Ralph held out the shard he had been carrying so long. I twisted it to make it work. Bea and Heidi looked over my shoulder.

Ralph took the shard from me and held it on a precise spot. "Right there."

"You are right. You are absolutely right."

I set the piece back on the table and four excited people sat down to dinner.

Sitting in the middle of the table was an amber bride's basket (Fig. 99) in the pattern known in the United States as *Shell and Tassel*. It sat in a silver-plated holder made by Meriden of Hamilton.

I should have known before. I had found on excavation at Burlington a broken half of a dog, and I knew the covered sugar and butter in this pattern had a finial in the form of a dog, lying with its head raised (Fig. 100). But that's often how it is—once a pattern is proven you think of many indicators you shouldn't have overlooked.

"You authenticated it, Ralph, but I'm going to name it." I said. "There is no way but that this can be known as anything else but *Hedlin Shell*."

All authentications are exciting but those are the three that I remember as being particularly gratifying. Two of them confirmed as being Canadian patterns—*Hedlin Shell* and *Button and Buckle*—are very handsome and are readily found in Canadian shops even today by the persistent collector. The pattern known as *Heidi* is likely to require a much longer search to collect but is well worth a major effort. It is very beautiful and illustrates three distinct processes in the making of Canadian glass. It is important.

The other patterns that we authenticated in the last five years I shall simply comment on briefly with the illustrations.

FIGURE 98 *A group of variants of the* Fleur-de-Lis *pattern in coloured glass. The bowl and nappies have* Rayed *bases. Burlington Glass Works, Hamilton, Ontario,* c. 1900.

FIGURE 99 *On the left is a pressed, honey-amber, footed dish in the* Button and Buckle *pattern. Three-piece mould, serrated rim. Height 4". Burlington Glass Works, Hamilton, Ontario, c. 1890.*

In the centre is a pressed, amber, footed dish in the Hedlin Shell *pattern. The Britannia-metal stand was silvered and manufactured by the Meriden Britannia Co., Hamilton, Ontario. Height of dish 4"; height of stand 11". Burlington Glass Works, c. 1890.*

On the right is a blue Button and Buckle *footed dish. Height 4"; diameter 8³/4".*

98

99

FIGURE 100 *Illustrated here are four pieces of the newly identified Canadian pattern which I have named* Hedlin Shell, *in recognition of my long-time students, Ralph and Heidi (Redekop) Hedlin, who worked so long and so hard to confirm its Canadian origins. Burlington Glass Works, Hamilton, Ontario, c. 1890.*

From left to right: a pressed, flint-glass, footed spooner (height 5⅛"); a pressed, flint-glass, footed sugar bowl with dog finial on the cover (height 6¾"); a pressed, flint-glass, footed butter dish with dog finial on the cover; a pressed, flint-glass, footed cream pitcher (height 5½"). Rare. Burlington Glass Works, c. 1890.

100

FIGURE 101 *A detail of the* Hedlin Shell *pattern, proven by shards to have been produced at the Burlington Glass Works, Hamilton, Ontario,* c. *1890.*

FIGURE 102 *From left to right: a pressed, flint-glass, footed celery (height 8⁵/₈"); a pressed, flint-glass, footed fruit dish made in a two-piece mould (height 8¹/₄"); a pressed, flint-glass, footed cake salver (height 5", width 8"). All in the* Hedlin Shell *pattern. Burlington Glass Works, Hamilton, Ontario,* c. *1890.*

101

102

FIGURE 103 *The two pieces on the left are in the newly identified* Hedlin Shell *pattern. The goblet was made of pressed flint glass in a three-piece mould (height 6³⁄₈″). The pressed, flint-glass, footed pitcher was made in a two-piece mould. Both from the Burlington Glass Works, Hamilton, Ontario, c. 1890.*

The two pieces on the right were made in the same factory at about the same time. Both are in the Daisy Band and Button *pattern. The pressed, flint-glass goblet was made in a two-piece mould.*

103

FIGURE 104 *On the left is a small platter in the* Hedlin Shell *pattern. Length 13¹/₈"; width 9". Burlington Glass Works, Hamilton, Ontario, c. 1890.*

In the centre is a pressed, flint-glass plate decorated with a Sheaf of Wheat *on the base, a* Rib *motif on the lower edge and the legend ''Give Us This Day Our Daily Bread'' is on the upper edge. Scalloped rim. Diameter 10".*

Authenticated by shards excavated at the site of the Burlington Glass Works. Circa 1890.

On the right is a pressed, flint-glass dish in the form of a fish. The legend on the base reads, ''Pat. June 1872.'' A white opal shard of this pattern was excavated at the Burlington site, but no clear flint shard was found. Circa 1880.

104

FIGURE 105 *Four pieces in the* Pleat and Panel *pattern. The cake salver in the centre background was made of pressed, flint glass (height 6⁷/₁₆″, width 9″). On the left is an octagonal, pressed, flint-glass condiment dish with pierced handles (height 1³/₈″, length 9⁵/₈″). In the centre foreground is a square (6″×6″), pressed, flint-glass dish. On the right is an octagonal dish in pressed flint glass (depth 2¹/₈″, length 8⁷/₈″, width 5¹/₂″).*

105

FIGURE 106 *A detail of the* Pleat and Panel *pattern proven by shards to have been made at the Burlington Glass Works, Hamilton, Ontario,* c. *1890.*

FIGURE 107 *The* Pleat and Panel *pattern illustrated here was identified as Canadian by shards excavated at the site of the Burlington Glass Works, Hamilton, Ontario. It was in production circa 1890.*

The octagonal, pressed, flint-glass tray has open handles (height 1¹/₈", length 13", width 8¹/₂"). In the centre is a pressed, flint-glass, footed, water pitcher (height 9³/₄"). On the right is a pressed, flint-glass, octagonal-footed dish (height 6³/₄").

106

107

FIGURE 108 *Shards excavated at the site of the Burlington Glass Works, Hamilton, Ontario, prove that the* Arch and Fan *pattern shown here on a pair of nappies was produced in Canada. The nappies were made in two-piece moulds (height 1¾"), c. 1890.*

FIGURE 109 *A detail of the* Arch and Fan *pattern made at the Burlington Glass Works, c. 1890.*

109

108

FIGURE 110 *The* Diamond Sunburst *pattern shown here is yet another new Canadian pattern proven by shards to have been produced at the Burlington Glass Works, Hamilton, Ontario, circa 1890.*

The footed candy dish on the left has a foot and base identical to the Sawtooth *example illustrated in Figure 223. Height 4⁵/₈"; diameter 6¹/₈".*

The pressed, flint-glass, footed bowl second from left has the Diamond Sunburst *motif on the base, bowl and cover. The base was made in a two-piece mould; cover in three-piece mould. Height 10³/₄".*

The footed, flint-glass goblet second from right was pressed in a three-piece mould. Height 6¹/₄".

The mould-blown, flint-glass syrup jar on the right has an applied handle with slight trailing. The pattern appears on the lower area, while the base has a Rayed *motif. Height 6".*

FIGURE 111 *Four pieces in the* Diamond Sunburst *pattern.*

On the left is a pressed, three-mould glass creamer. The foot and design area are commonplace; however, the upper area and lip have been hand worked. The applied handle with slight trailing adds much to the appeal of a far from commonplace example of early Canadian glass. Height 6³/8″.

In the centre background is a pressed, three-mould glass spooner. Height 5¹/4″.

On the right is a footed celery pressed in a three-piece mould. The lower area is not unique; however, the upper area with its hand-worked, gently serrated rim is quite attractive.

In the centre foreground is a pressed, flint-glass relish dish with a Rayed *base. Length 9³/8″.*

111

FIGURE 112 *Three fascinating examples of the* Fleur-de-Lis *pattern. On the left is a cake salver (height 4½", diameter 9⅛"); in the centre is a vase made in a four-piece mould with four-point fluted lip (height 10¾", width 3/4").*

The pressed, flint-glass salver on the right is extremely interesting and may be classed as rare. The plate area has been reheated and bent in a semi-circular form which is seldom encountered in Canadian glass. The motifs are many and include the Fleur-de-Lis. *Pressed in a four-piece mould. Height 7³/₁₆".*

FIGURE 113 *On the left is a mug with handle (height 3¼", diameter 2¾"); in the centre is a covered sugar with handles of ribbed design (overall height 6"; diameter, including handles, 6"); on the right is a spooner with handles (height 4", diameter 6").*

The fluted top of the sugar fits inside the bowl, and it has a Fleur-de-Lis *finial.*

112

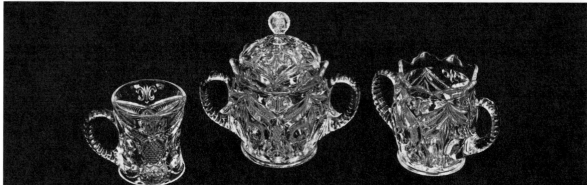

113

FIGURE 114 *The* Fleur-de-Lis *pattern illustrated here was made at the Burlington Glass Works, Hamilton, Ontario, between about 1890 and 1900.*

From left to right: the bowl measures 5" high and 8³/₈" wide, the covered sugar 6¹/₄" high and 5" wide, and the biscuit jar 8" high and 5" wide.

This pattern was made in several Canadian glass factories. Care should be exercised by the collector, as the pattern has been continued and many pieces have been machine made in more recent years.

FIGURE 115 *A detail of the* Fleur-de-Lis *finial on the biscuit jar shown in Figure 114.*

115

114

FIGURE 116 *Another detail of the* Fleur-de-Lis *pattern which was produced at Burlington and several other Canadian glass factories.*

FIGURE 117 *A* Fleur-de-Lis *handled relish dish (height 1³/4", diameter 5") and shallow dish (depth 1³/4", diameter 10¹/4").*

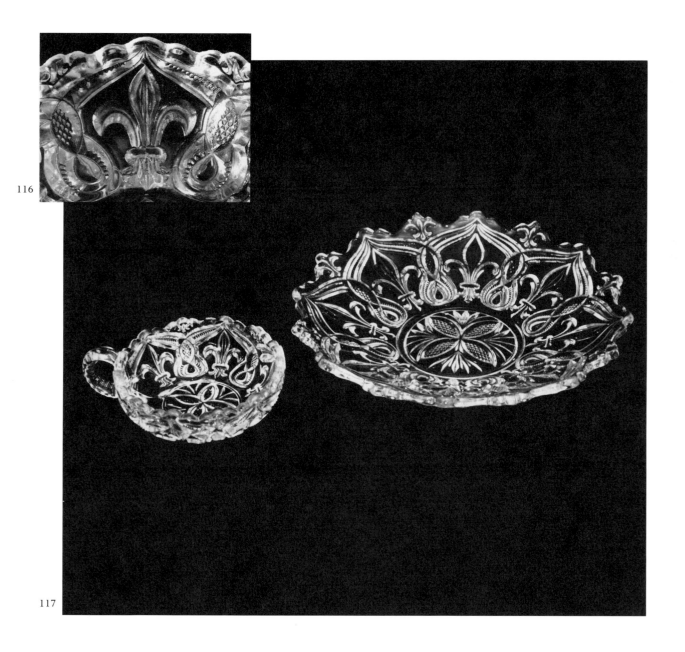

116

117

FIGURE 118 *Three examples of the* Button and Buckle *pattern. On the left is a pressed, flint-glass, footed water jug with handle made in a three-piece mould (height 7³/4"; diameter, including spout and handle, 7³/4"). In the foreground is a pressed, flint-glass, footed nappy with a serrated edge (height 2³/8"). On the right is a pressed, flint-glass, footed bowl with a serrated edge (height 4¹/2", diameter 8¹/2"). All from the Burlington Glass Works, Hamilton, Ontario,* c. 1890.

FIGURE 119 *A detail of the* Button and Buckle *pattern proven by shards to be a product of the Burlington Glass Works,* c. 1890.

119

FIGURE 120 *On the left is a pressed, flint-glass covered butter dish a variant of the* Daisy Band and Button *pattern with a* Daisy *motif on the finial (height 7", diameter 6¹/8". Beside it is a matching creamer (height 5"; diameter including lip and handle, 5¹/2").*

In the foreground is a covered butter dish decorated with a variant of the Daisy Band and Button *pattern (height, including finial, 5¹/2"; width 5¹/8").*

On the right is a pressed, flint-glass spooner with Daisy Band and Button *motifs,* Rayed *base and scalloped lip (height 4¹-2", diameter 3¹/8").*

FIGURE 121 *Illustrations of the* Button and Buckle *pattern authenticated as Canadian by shards found at the site of the Burlington Glass Works, Hamilton, Ontario. These pieces were produced* circa 1890.

On the left is a pressed, clear flint-glass, footed spooner made in a three-piece mould. Height 5¹/4"; diameter 3⁷/16".

Second from left is a pressed, clear flint-glass, footed, covered sugar made in a three-piece mould. Overall height 7¹/4"; diameter 4¹/8".

Second from right is a pressed, flint-glass, footed butter dish with cover. Base and cover pressed in three-piece moulds. The finial has Button, Buckle *and* Ray *motifs. Height 5¹/2"; diameter 5¹/2".*

On the right is a pressed, flint-glass, footed creamer with a scalloped pouring spout made in a three-piece mould. Height 5¹/4"; diameter (including handle) 5¹/8".

118

120

12

FIGURE 122 *An etched* Daisy Band and Button *cake salver. Height 7" diameter 9³/₈". Burlington Glass Works, Hamilton, Ontario,* c. *1890.*

FIGURE 123 *Detail of the goblet in the* Daisy Band and Button *pattern authenticated as Canadian by shards found at the site of the Burlington Glass Works.*

FIGURE 124 *Three pieces decorated in the* Daisy Band and Button *pattern produced by the Burlington Glass Works, Hamilton, Ontario,* c. *1900.*

On the left is a pressed, flint-glass nappy with Daisy Band and Button *skirt,* Block and Starred Block *band, serrated edge, and* Rayed *base.*

In the centre is a pressed, flint-glass, footed dish and cover. Rayed base and cover; Block and Cross *finial. Height 11¹/₄".*

On the right is a pressed, flint-glass covered butter dish. Height (including finial) 6¹/₂"; width 5".

123

122

FIGURE 125 *The two pieces shown here and those in the following illustration are in the* Heidi Daisy and Button *pattern. Authenticated by George Gardiner and by Burlington shards, this pattern illustrates pressing, acid-etching and cutting. It is very rare, one of Burlington's most beautiful creations.*

In recognition of months of dedicated searching for new patterns, I have named it after Heidi Redekop (Hedlin). All six pieces were made at the Burlington Glass Works, Hamilton, Ontario, circa 1885.

On the left is a pressed, flint-glass, footed bowl with cover. The cover has a six-sided finial and Daisy and Button *motif. The lower area was rendered opaque by the use of acid, then wheel-engraved to clear in a geometric design. The upper area of the bowl is of* Daisy and Button *design, the lower area is opaque and wheel-engraved. The pressed base shows the same motif and is applied to the bowl. Height 11½".*

On the right is a pressed, flint-glass water pitcher with applied handle in the Heidi Daisy and Button *pattern. Opaque body with wheel-engraved geometric motifs. The lip has been worked. The applied handle was twisted in a technique much favoured by the Burlington glassblowers and identified by shards found at the factory site. Height at lip 7¾".*

125

FIGURE 126 *Four more pieces in the newly identified and named* Heidi Daisy and Button. *Refer to the preceding illustration for two other pieces of the same set.*

On the left is a spooner in pressed flint-glass. Height 5".

Second from left is a covered butter dish. The exterior of the base and rim are decorated with the Daisy and Button *motif. Overall height 5⅝"; diameter of base 7¼".*

Second from right is a covered sugar bowl in pressed flint-glass. Overall height 8⅛".

On the right is a pressed, flint-glass pitcher with an applied handle in a rope design. Height 5".

FIGURE 127 *Four shards excavated at the site of the Burlington Glass Works, Hamilton, Ontario. Upper and lower left:* Daisy Band and Button. *Upper right:* Sheaf of Wheat bread plate. *Lower right: opal glass fish plate.*

FIGURE 128 *Additional shards from the Burlington site. Upper left:* Button and Buckle. *Lower left:* Pleat and Panel. *Centre:* Button Ladder. *Upper right:* Arch and Fan. *Lower right:* Hedlin Shell.

127

128

FIGURE 129 *A detail of the* But-ton Ladder *pattern proven by shards as being produced at the Burlington Glass Works, c. 1890.*

FIGURE 130 *Shards unearthed at the site of the Burlington Glass Works, Hamilton, Ontario, identify* Button Ladder *as a Canadian pattern made at Burlington,* circa *1890.*

The Button Ladder *creamer on the left is in pressed flint-glass. Made in a three-piece mould and with an applied handle. Height 5½".*

The goblet is in pressed flint-glass. Made in a three-piece mould. Height 5¾".

129

130

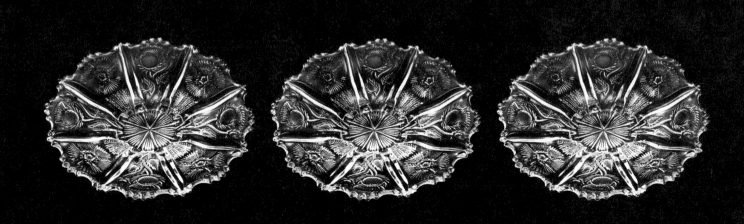

PRESSED GLASS

THIS IS AN INTERVIEW between George Arthur Shakely, who worked in the Jefferson Glass Company, Toronto, Ontario, from 1912, and Gerald Stevens. It took place in the Toronto home of Mr. Shakely in 1959.

G.S.: Mr. Shakely, I understand that you were a glassblower. Would you recount some of your early reminiscences?

G.A.S.: Well, I went to work when I was a child, you know. A boy.

G.S.: At what age?

G.A.S.: Twelve.

G.S.: What were your duties at the age of twelve?

G.A.S.: What we called carrying-in and snapping-up for the blowers.

G.S.: What does carrying-in mean?

G.A.S.: I carried the hot glass on an iron fork and put it in a tempering oven.

G.S.: And from there?

G.A.S.: We worked at that four or five years. Then they took me on as an apprentice working in the glass factory. That's working on hot metal.

G.S.: That's a point I would like to clear up. Before being an apprentice one had to be associated with the glass factory and be a carrying-in-boy or a helper of some sort?

G.A.S.: That's for sure. We wouldn't let anyone come in there and jump ahead of us. At that time the glass trade was good, and everybody who could stand it was trying to get a place in the trade.

G.S.: How long did you serve as an apprentice before you became a qualified glassblower?

G.A.S.: I'd say seven years to be really qualified, although we worked four years as an apprentice. I went to work at the trade when I was seventeen. I was twenty-one when they took me in the union.

G.S.: In other words, in four years you really became a qualified glassblower?

G.A.S.: Well, yes, but you learn more as you go on, you know.

G.S.: The term "glassblower" in your case, what did it constitute? What was your work?

G.A.S.: My work was mostly on fruit jars, lantern globes. Shades began to come in then, electric shades. I worked for a long time on shades.

G.S.: When did you first come to Canada?

G.A.S.: 1911.

G.S.: What firm were you with at that time?

G.A.S.: At that time it was called Lowden Brothers. I don't know for how long it had been called that. It was so long ago. In 1912 we shut down in the spring and we shut down all summer. We remodelled the furnace, and made it look like a new factory altogether. It was called the Jefferson Glass Company from then on.

G.S.: Did they usually shut down the glasshouse in July and August? Is it correct that the heat was so great that the factories closed?

G.A.S.: It was really hot. I think most of them closed down for five or six weeks.

G.S.: During the period of your working in Toronto, what did the glass house produce? What were their commercial wares?

G.A.S.: Bottles and tableware. And I was on tableware. We made anything that goes on the table.

G.S.: Was the tableware blown or was it pressed?

G.A.S.: Mostly pressed.

G.S.: How was the gather obtained from which the specific piece of tableware would be made? Was it obtained by a blow pipe or was it more or less automatic?

G.A.S.: For the gather on tableware you had a presser. He would gather out of the pot. They used pots, they didn't have any tanks. We'd gather on what we'd call the punty. We'd get that hot glass off that punty in the mould and in the presser. Then we'd cut it off.* Snipped it with a pair of scissors. I've got my shears yet.

---

* When the cold metal of the shears met the glass some crystallization always occurred at the cut. In determining whether glass was hand pressed, and so was probably "of the period," the collector should always look for a scar or line in the glass. The presence of this scar confirms that the gather from which the particular piece of glass product was made was snipped with the glassmaker's shears and was not machine made. The line may be anywhere on the piece, it may be on the surface or embedded in the glass. On a very occasional piece it might have been polished out, but the odds against this are high. G.S.

G.S.: You say drop it in the mould and then the pressure was applied. Was the pressure mechanical or was it applied by a man?

G.A.S.: The pressing was done by a presser—a man. The presser put the mould back in the press under the plunger. Then he pulled a lever down that made the article: tumblers, spoon holders, sugar bowls, butter dishes and all that sort of thing.

G.S.: Did these pieces have designs on them?

G.A.S.: They had figures. There were all kinds of designs cut in the mould. The plunger was plain, and formed a smooth inside of the sugar bowl, or whatever we were making. The outside or bottom of the piece was figured from the mould, so that's how the design would come out, don't you know.

G.S.: I notice that one of the designs, we are looking at it now, is one that is known as *Crystal* in the States.

G.A.S.: That's right. That's actually *Chippendale.** We made it at Jefferson, and that is what we called it.

G.S.: You made a lot of commercial products at Jefferson. How about the pieces that we call whimseys—paperweights, glass hats, canes and all that sort of thing? Was anything like that made at Jefferson Glass Works?

G.A.S.: We wouldn't make stuff like that to sell. We made that as a hobby. I made a bunch of them. Gave them away as fast as I made them.

G.S.: What types did you make?

G.A.S.: I made glass hats. They called them derbies at that time, you know. You make them out of spoon holders or tumblers.

G.S.: How would you go about turning a tumbler into a glass hat?

G.A.S.: You would get it really hot. They were stuck up—dab up—on what they called those snapping punties. The same with a gathering punty. We'd heat them in what we call the glory hole, really fiery hot. Then I'd bring it out and do the work on a finishing chair with a finishing tool.

G.S.: What did the finishing tool look like?

G.A.S.: It opened up like a pair of scissors.

G.S.: Would it be something similar to a sugar tong?

---

* In *Canadian Glass c1825-1925* I called the No. 1600 design (pages 164, 165, 181-183) *Colonial.* It was sold by Jefferson as *Chippendale*, and to be correct, that is what it should be called.

G.A.S.: Something like. It had a spring handle on it, that opens it. First the tumbler was pressed you know. I would shape it up and I would make a cap or a hat.

G.S.: You made caps as well as hats?

G.A.S.: Yes, I did myself. A lot of them would stand around watching me do it. It's given to you. You have to be a glassworker to pick things up like that.

G.S.: I understand. You also made paperweights?

G.A.S.: Yes.

G.S.: Could you describe your operations in making a paperweight?

G.A.S.: The first thing you do in making a paperweight is gather a piece of hot glass on a punty. You shape it up in a finishing chair with a wooden paddle. Then you would have your coloured glass laying down on an iron plate, and you would take that hot glass on that punty and dab it on your coloured glass. The coloured glass is in small pieces and they would stick to the hot glass. Then you would shape that up in a finishing chair with that wooden paddle. The finisher would do this himself. He would go to the pot and cover the whole business with hot glass again. Then I would take it back to the finishing chair and finish it and smooth it up. There's your paper-weight. But you would have to put that in the oven because, if you didn't temper it, it would fly all to pieces.

G.S.: Tempering? That would be in the annealing oven?

G.A.S.: That's right.

G.S.: When the first gather of glass was touched to the coloured glass, was the coloured glass hot?

G.A.S.: No, you didn't have to heat it. The coloured glass would not be very big pieces. You leave it lay on an iron plate and you dab that hot glass down on it and just leave it for three or four seconds. The coloured glass would be thin and would heat through mighty quick to the hot molten glass. It would stick. You would cover it again, go over to the pot of hot glass and cover it all over again.

G.S.: Where did you obtain the coloured pieces?

G.A.S.: We made coloured glass in different pots. Little pieces of coloured glass would be laying around. You'd pick them up.

G.S.: I notice in this paperweight made by yourself there is blue and red. Were those colours made in the Jefferson glasshouse or were they imported?

G.A.S.: Some of the colours were imported. But I got some colours myself. You only need a pocketful. You would make a hundred paperweights out of that.

G.S.: I understand the Lowden Brothers had one glassmaker who really knew how to obtain very fine colours in glass.

G.A.S.: His name was Wit. He was good. Lowden came after that. Lowden Brothers didn't carry the same manager when the Jefferson started. Jefferson had a different manager.

G.S.: And different glassmakers?

G.A.S.: That's right.

G.S.: Besides hats and paperweights, what other types of whimsey did you make?

G.A.S.: Glass canes.

G.S.: What size were these?

G.A.S.: Natural size.

G.S.: And what colours would you use?

G.A.S.: Any colour glass they wanted, all colours. I'd put different colours in there and twist the cane and the colours would twist up. If I had any here I'd give you one, but we haven't any. We'd give them away as fast as we'd make them.

G.S.: Were the canes perfectly tubular or were they twisted when you were finished?

G.A.S.: The coloured glass in them was twisted around but the whole thing was smooth on the outside.

G.S.: Did you ever see any canes made that had a twisted appearance on the outer body itself?

G.A.S.: Not that I know of.

G.S.: As well as paperweights, hats and canes, I understand that you made watch chains from glass of different colours. Did you make many of these?

G.A.S.: Hundreds of them.* But I'd give them away as fast as I'd make them. Everybody would want one. It took me some time to make them.

G.S.: What was the usual size or length of the link?

G.A.S.: Around a half an inch.

---

* Collectors should be alert with respect to these glass watch chains. I know of no one else, other than George Shakely, who made them, and according to his testimony he made "hundreds of them." Any found should, if possible, be traced. It would be very important if they could be traced back to Mr. Shakely.

G.S.: And it would be long enough to go across the vest, and there was an additional piece to which the watch was attached. Is that correct?

G.A.S.: That is right.

G.S.: Did many other people make these watch chains?

G.A.S.: I never seen anyone else make one at all. They would always come to me for a watch chain.

G.S.: As far as I know you are the only Canadian glassblower to make watch chains. I wish to thank you Mr. Shakely for this interview. You've been very kind and very generous with your reminiscences.

G.A.S.: That's fine.

FIGURE 131 *The blown, three-mould, blue opal salt on the left has a* Cross *motif. Height 3¹/8". Authenticated by shards excavated at the site of the Burlington Glass Works, Hamilton, Ontario.* Circa *1880.*

The blown, three-mould white opal salt second from left has a Circle and Leaf *motif. Height 3". Burlington Glass Works, c. 1880.*

In the centre is a blown, two-mould, blue opal salt in a Horseshoe *motif. Height 3¹/2". Burlington Glass Works, c. 1880.*

The salt shown second from right was blown in a two-piece mould with white-opal overlay on flint. Height 3". Authenticated by shards excavated at the Burlington Glass Works. Circa *1880.*

The blown, four-mould, blue opal salt on the right has a Swirl *motif. Height 2¹/2". Burlington Glass Works, c. 1880.*

FIGURE 132 *On the left is a very rare mould-blown, amberina (amber to ruby) glass salt decorated with six* Fleur-de-Lis *motifs. Three-piece mould; Brittania-metal top. Height 2³/4" (breaking away the blowpipe results in minor variations in height). Burlington Glass Works, Hamilton, Ontario, c. 1890.*

On the right is an equally rare salt mould-blown in ruby glass and decorated with six Fleur-de-Lis *motifs. Acid dipped to the shoulder and painted with floral motifs. Three-piece mould; Brittania-metal top. Shards of this colour and motif were excavated at the Burlington site.* Circa *1890.*

Perhaps the real authority on these distinctive Burlington salts is my wife, Bea. Although we worked together in authenticating them, she is the one who looked through every display and scoured the back rooms of shops to assemble the unique collection of Canadian salts that follows. G.S.

FIGURE 133 *The pair of shakers on the left of the illustration is in pressed blue glass.* Diamond Quilted *motifs;* Rayed *bases; two-piece moulds. Height 2¹/2". Burlington Glass Works, Hamilton, Ontario, c. 1900.*

The shakers in the centre are mould-blown, two-mould, blue-opal glass. Canadian Moon and Star *motifs. Height 2¹/2". Authenticated by shards excavated at the Burlington site.* Circa *1880.*

The Canadian Shell *motif decorates the pair on the right. Blown, three-mould opal glass. The shells have been coloured. Authenticated by shards from the Burlington site.* Circa *1880.*

131

132

133

FIGURE 134 *Shown here is a bride's basket in pale green with flutted and scalloped edges. Height 3³/₄″; diameter 11¹/₂″. The silver-plated stand was made by Meriden, Hamilton, Ontario.*

134

FIGURE 135 *The carafe in the centre of this illustration was mould-blown in lead glass and decorated in the* Colonial *pattern. The body is decorated with designs illustrating needle etching techniques. Polished rim. Height 10". Dominion Glass, Montreal, Wallaceburg, Toronto, etc., c. 1915-25.*

The wines in the background are (left to right): flint-glass, needle-etched, Dominion Glass Company, Montreal, c. 1910; flint glass, wheel-engraved, Foster Brothers Glass Works, St. Johns, P.Q., c. 1875; lead glass, needle-etched, Dominion Glass Company, Montreal, c. 1910.

The piece in the left foreground is a juice glass made on an automatic machine, then needle-etched with fleurs-de-lis. *Lead glass. Height 3½". Dominion Glass Company, c. 1915-1925.*

FIGURE 136 *The* Oak Leaf *and inverted* Fleur-de-Lis *motif characterizes the white and blue opal salts shown on the left. Each one was blown in a two-piece mould and has ''No. 2'' imprinted on the base. Height 2³⁄₄". Both types authenticated by shards excavated at the site of the Burlington Glass Works, Hamilton, Ontario. Circa 1880.*

The Princess Feather *motif characterizes the white and blue opal salts shown in the centre. Each one was blown in a four-piece mould. Height 3". The blue piece was authenticated by shards, and both were made at the Burlington Glass Works, c. 1880.*

The Tassel *motif characterizes the blue and white opal salts on the right. Each one was blown in a four-piece mould. Height 2¹⁄₂". The piece on the far right was authenticated by shards, and both were made at the Burlington Glass Works, c. 1880.*

136

FIGURE 137 *On the left is a blown, three-mould, blue opal salt. Burlington Flute motif. Height 3⅛" Burlington Glass Works, Hamilton, Ontario, c. 1890.*

Second from left is a blown, four-mould, blue opal salt in the Corn *motif. Height 3".*

The blown, three-mould, pale green opal salt second from right is imprinted ''Hamilton, Ont.'' Height 2⅜". Burlington Glass Works, c. 1895.

The blown, two-mould opal salt on the right has a Butterfly and Tassel *motif. Height 3". Burlington Glass Works, c. 1880.*

FIGURE 138 *Pressed, opal-covered bowls in white and blue. Made in three-piece moulds and with the numeral ''5'' on cover and base. The piece on the right has a painted floral motif and the legend, ''With compliments D. S. Mallory, Mallorytown.'' However, neither of these bowls was made in Mallorytown. Heights 2⅝"; diameters 3⁵⁄₁₆". Burlington, Glass Works, Hamilton, Ontario, c. 1890.*

137

138

FIGURE 139 *Three pairs of shakers from the Burlington Glass Works, Hamilton, Ontario.*

On the left is a pair of blown, four-mould, white opal shakers with Filigree *motifs. Height 3⁵/₈"; c. 1880.*

In the centre is a pair of blown, four-mould opal shakers in the "No. 7" pattern. Height 3¹/₂". The piece on the left was authenticated by shards excavated on the site; the one on the right is a variant. Circa *1880.*

On the far right is a pair of blown, four-mould, opal shakers in the Swirl *motif. Height 2¹/₂". Authenticated by shards.* Circa *1880.*

139

FIGURE 140 *Five salts and peppers from the Burlington Glass Works, Hamilton, Ontario.*

The salt on the far left is of opal glass blown in a two-piece mould. Enameled floral motif and tole top. Height 3⁵/₈″. Circa 1885.

The three-piece set second from left includes mould-blown, opal salt and pepper shakers made at Burlington in two-piece moulds and a Brittania-metal stand with the legend ''Made and guaranteed by Meriden Company [in cir-

cular mark]—Hamilton, Canada.'' Height of salt and pepper 4¹/₄″; height of stand 7″. Circa 1890.

Second from right is a blown, three-mould opal salt with an enameled floral motif and Brittania-metal top. Height 3⁵/₈″. Circa 1885.

On the right is a blown, two-mould opal salt with an enameled floral motif and Brittania-metal top. Circa 1885.

FIGURE 141 Greek Key *and* Interlocking Ring *motifs decorate these three pieces. The opalescent and clear glass jug measures 8" high, diameter 5" (see* Early Canadian Glass, *p. 62). The amber and white opal dish with serrated edge in the centre measures 4¼" in diameter, as does the blue and white opal example on the right. Both are from the Burlington Glass Works, Hamilton, Ontario, c. 1895.*

141

FIGURE 142 *On the left is a blown, two-mould syrup jug of blue glass decorated with a* Coin Dot *design. Swirl foot, applied handle, Britannia-metal top. Height 6¾". Burlington Glass Works, Hamilton, Ontario, c. 1885.*

The green glass wine in the centre has the Grape and Vine *motif. Four-piece mould. Height 4⅛". Sydenham Glass Company, Wallaceburg, Ontario, c. 1910.*

The pressed, flint-glass goblet was made in a four-piece mould. Eight Block *motifs with ruby flashing on them and the rim. Authenticated as Canadian by shards excavated at the site of the Burlington Glass Works, Hamilton, Ontario. Circa 1890.*

FIGURE 143 *On the left is a pressed, opal miniature tray with* Greek Lyre and Dart *motifs. Mould-blown salt and pepper made in four-piece moulds and with vining motifs. Burlington Glass Works, Hamilton, Ontario, c. 1885.*

On the right is a set with a pressed, opal tray with a mould-blown salt and pepper. Fleur-de-Lis *and additional motifs. Height of pepper 3¹/₈". Burlington Glass Works, c. 1885.*

FIGURE 144 *The pair of opal glass shakers on the left was blown in three-piece moulds. Each piece has three* Fleur-de-Lis *motifs. Shards excavated on the site of the Burlington Glass Works, Hamilton, Ontario. Circa 1890.*

In the centre is a machine blown, two-piece mould, opal-glass salt or pepper shaker. Dominion Glass Company, Toronto, Ontario, c. 1920.

On the right is a pair of opal-glass Athenian *shakers; three-piece moulds. Height 2³/₄". Burlington Glass Works, and elsewhere, c. 1890.*

FIGURE 145 *The pair of shakers on the left was blown of opal glass in four-piece moulds.* Beaded Lattice and Frame *motifs. Height 3³/₈". Authenticated by shards found at the Burlington Glass Works, Hamilton Ontario. Circa 1880.*

The shakers on the right were blown of opal glass in four-piece moulds with Corn *motifs; height 3". The pressed, opal-glass stand was made in a two-piece mould. Authenticated by shards excavated at the Burlington Glass Works. Circa 1880.*

144

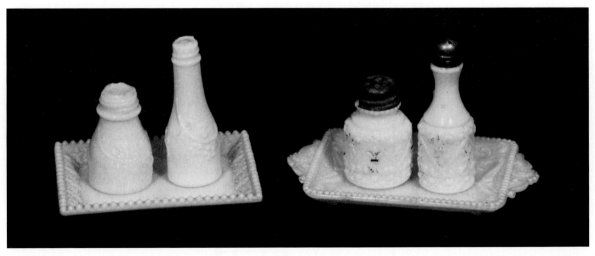

143

14⁴

14⁵

FIGURE 146 *The blue-coloured, flint-glass tumbler on the left is in the* Early Nugget *motif. Pressed in a four-piece mould. Sydenham Glass Company, Wallaceburg, Ontario, c. 1895.*

Second from left is a pressed, pale blue glass tumbler in the Colonial *pattern. Rayed base. Height 3½". Dominion Glass Company, Wallaceburg, Ontario, or Montreal, Quebec, c. 1920.*

Third from left is a pressed, marble-glass tumbler in Fleur-de-Lis *and floral motifs. Rayed base. Three-piece mould. Height 3⅞". Burlington Glass Works, Hamilton, Ontario, c. 1890.*

On the right is a Thousand-Eye *tumbler in pressed, blue flint glass. Height 3⅞".*

FIGURE 147 *The pressed, flint-glass tumbler on the left is in the* Block *pattern. Ruby flashing on blocks and rim. Four-piece mould. Height 3⅞". Shards excavated at the site of the Burlington Glass Works, Hamilton, Ontario. Circa 1890.*

Second from left is a pressed, amber glass tumbler. The Button and Buckle *motif appears on the side and base. Three-piece mould. Height 3¾". Burlington Glass Works, c. 1890.*

The Grape *design decorates the pressed, green glass tumbler third from left. Rayed base. Four-piece mould. Sydenham Glass Company, Wallaceburg, Ontario, c. 1890.*

The Daisy and Depressed Button *pattern appears on the pressed, flint, deep amber tumbler on the right. Height 3¾".*

FIGURE 148 *On the left is a covered butter dish and on the right a spooner in the dark green flint* Maple Leaf *pattern. Quebec and Ontario, c. 1890-1915.*

146

148

47

FIGURE 149 *In the foreground of this illustration is a miniature oblong tray in pressed, white-opal glass with handles and beaded edge. The design on the base includes a* Rayed Circle *and* Sawtooth *motif, while the top has a* Fleur-de-Lis *motif. Length 5¼"; width 3⅛". See* Canadian Glass c. 1825-1925, *p. 219.*

On the left is a pair of shakers in opal glass blown in four-piece moulds. Frame *and* Shell *motifs; imprinted ''No. 8'' on bases. Height 3⅝". Shards excavated on the site of the Burlington Glass Works, Hamilton, Ontario. Circa 1880.*

The pair on the right was blown of opal glass in two-piece moulds. Butterfly *and* Tassel *motifs. Height 3". Shards excavated on the Burlington site. Circa 1880.*

FIGURE 150 *On the left is a pair of mould-blown, flint-glass shakers in the* Block *motif. Four-piece moulds. Height 2⅞". Burlington Glass Works, Hamilton, Ontario, c. 1890.*

Beside this pair is a machine-blown, two-mould, flint-glass shaker designed as a ''Special Celery Salt.'' Height 5¾". Dominion Glass Company, Toronto, Ontario, c. 1925.

The second pair from the left is in pressed flint-glass with the Athenian *pattern. Three-piece moulds. Height 2¾". Burlington Glass Works, c. 1890.*

The pair on the right is in the Woodrow *pattern. Pressed flint-glass; three-piece moulds. Jefferson Glass Company, c. 1925.*

149

FIGURE 151 *Pressed, three-mould goblets in the* Button and Buckle *pattern were produced in medium, dark and honey amber, as well as blue and clear glass. Heights 6". Burlington Glass Works, Hamilton, Ontario, c. 1885.*

FIGURE 152 *All* Maple Leaf *tea sets, including those in flint glass, consist of the four items illustrated in white opal in Figure 266. The set shown here is made of blue opal.*

Left to right: creamer, covered butter dish and spooner. The cover is for the missing sugar. Quebec and Ontario, c. 1890-1915.

FIGURE 153 *Two pieces in the* Late Nugget *pattern. The creamer was pressed in a four-piece mould. Height 4¹/₂". The Sydenham Glass Company, Wallaceburg, Ontario, c. 1900.*

The green glass butter dish and cover measure 4¹/₂". Sydenham Glass Company, c. 1900.

51

153

FIGURE 154 *Shown here is a pressed, flint-glass* Beaver *goblet made in a three-piece mould. Motifs include beavers, maple leaves and the legend "St. Jean Baptiste—Quebec, 24 Juin 1880." Height 5⁵/₁₆". Excelsior Glass Company, St. Johns, Quebec, 1880.*

FIGURE 155 *This pressed, flint-glass goblet was made in a three-piece mould and decorated with the* Fleur-de-Lis *motif. Height 5³/₄". Authenticated by shards found at the Burlington Glass Works, Hamilton, Ontario. Made* circa. *1890.*

154

155

FIGURE 156 *A group of pieces in the* New York *or* Honeycomb *pattern.*

On the left is a pressed, flint-glass, lamp made from a honeycomb goblet. Not a plentiful item. Height 6³/₈". See Canadian Glass c. 1825-1925, p. 52.

The goblets beside the lamp were made in two-piece moulds. Height 5³/₄". Burlington Glass Works, Hamilton, Ontario, c. 1895.

The sherries and winers on the right of the illustration were also made at Burlington, c. 1895.

156

FIGURE 157 *On the left is a pressed, flint-glass, three-mould goblet in the 101 pattern. Height 5⁷⁄₈". Burlington Glass Works, Hamilton, Ontario, c. 1890.*

The centre piece is a pressed, flint-glass, four-mould goblet in the Rayed Heart *pattern. Height 5³⁄₄". Jefferson Glass Company, Toronto, Ontario, c. 1915.*

On the right is a pressed, flint-glass, three-mould goblet in the Palmette *pattern. Height 6¹⁄₈". Burlington Glass Works, c. 1890.*

157

FIGURE 158 *The two pieces on the left are in the* Sawtooth *pattern. Wine height 4½″; goblet height 6⅜″. Burlington Glass Works, Hamilton, Ontario, c. 1890.*

On the right are two pieces in the Block *motif. Height of wine 4⅛″; height of goblet 5¾″. Burlington Glass Works, c. 1890.*

158

FIGURE 159 *This flint glass goblet was wheel-engraved with initials, floral motifs and on one side "Dr. J.A." and on the other "From A Friend 1879." This interesting and important goblet is from the same mould as the "C.D.A. Exhibition" goblet illustrated on page 122 of* Early Canadian Glass. *This example provides evidence that such goblets were engraved on special order and so opens up an interesting area for further investigation and collecting. Height 6¹/₁₆". Excelsior Glass Company, St. John's, P.Q., 1878-1880.*

FIGURE 160 *The Burlington Glass Works, Hamilton, Ontario, was the source of these three pieces in the* Dominion *pattern. Shards matching the goblet were found on the site. All were made* circa *1890.*

The wine on the far right matches the one next to it, except that the upper portion has been needle-etched.

159

160

FIGURE 161 *A group of pressed, flint-glass goblets from the Foster Brothers Glass Works, St. Johns, P.Q., all made* circa *1875. The first and third from the left have been wheel-engraved.*

161

FIGURE 162 *Four goblets made in Trenton, Nova Scotia, circa 1890, all in three-piece moulds. The patterns are (left to right):* Raspberry and Shield *(height 6¼")*, Nova Scotia Diamond *(height 6")*, Nova Scotia Star Flower *(height 6")*, Nova Scotia Rib Band *(height 6⅛")*.

FIGURE 163 *A group of pieces decorated with the* Colonial (Chippendale) *pattern, all from the Jefferson Glass Company, Toronto, Ontario, c. 1915. See* Canadian Glass c. 1825-1925, *pps. 164-167.*

Left to right: two-mould wine (height 4"); two-mould sundae dish; two-mould wine (height 4"); two-mould goblet (height 6⅛"); two-mould wine (height 3⅞"); two-mould wine.

162

163

FIGURE 164 *On the left is a pressed, flint-glass, two-mould goblet in the* New York *pattern. Height 5"; diameter 2⅛". Burlington Glass Works, Hamilton, Ontario, c. 1895.*

Second from left is a pressed, flint-glass goblet in Button and Bows *motif with a broad base. Height 6"; diameter of lip 2½"; diameter of base 3¹/₁₆". Nova Scotia; see George Mac-Laren,* Nova Scotia Glass, *p. 33.*

Second from right is a pressed, flint-glass, three-mould goblet in the Cross *pattern. Height 5⅞". Burlington Glass Works, c. 1890.*

On the right is a pressed, flint-glass, three-mould goblet with a Pointed Bull's-Eye *motif. Height 6". Burlington Glass Works, c. 1895.*

164

FIGURE 165 *Four goblets made in Trenton, Nova Scotia, c. 1890. Left to right: three-mould,* Nova Scotia Kenlee *motif (height 5⅞"); three-mould,* Nova Scotia Gothic *motif (height 6⅛"); four-mould,* Pillar *pattern, wheel-engraved floral motifs (height 6⅛"); three-mould,* Nova Scotia Grape and Vine *motif (height 6").*

FIGURE 166 *The pressed, flint-glass goblets illustrated here were made in Trenton, Nova Scotia, c. 1890. Left to right: three-mould,* Raspberry *pattern (height 5¾"); three-mould,* Nova Scotia Tandem *motif (height 5⅝"); three-mould,* Nova Scotia Floral *pattern (height 6"); four-mould,* Nova Scotia Ribbon and Star *motif (height 5⅞").*

165

166

FIGURE 167 *In about 1925 the Jefferson Glass Company, Toronto, Ontario, produced these pressed, flint-glass pieces in the* Daisy and X-Band *pattern.*

The miniature open sugar and creamer on the left were made in four-piece moulds. Height 2¼".

The goblet and wine were also made in four-piece moulds. Both show the pattern on the bowl and base.

167

FIGURE 168 *These two pieces were free-blown, not pressed. A comparison of this illustration with others in the chapter will reveal the differences between the two techniques.*

The lead-glass wine on the left has a folded rim on the foot and a scar indicating the use of a blowpipe. A non-commercial item. Height 3½". Diamond Glass Company, Montreal, P.Q., c. 1890.

On the right is a one-of-a-kind, free-blown, lead-glass tumbler. Wheel-cut and engraved with floral and geometric motifs. Ground pontil mark. Height 3⅞". St. Lawrence Glass Company, Montreal, c. 1868.

FIGURE 169 *A group of pressed, flint-glass goblets in (left to right):* Hedlin Shell, Pleat and Panel, Daisy Band and Button, *and* Button and Buckle. *Shown here for reference, these newly authenticated Canadian patterns are discussed more fully in Chapter 5.*

FIGURE 170 *The pressed, flint-glass wine on the left is decorated in the* Daisy and Depressed Button *pattern. Height 4".*

Second from left is a pressed, flint-glass, three-mould wine with the Diamond Sunburst *motif. Burlington Glass Works, Hamilton, Ontario, c. 1890.*

The Daisy and Depressed Button *goblet was pressed in a three-piece mould. This particular item is being extensively copied. Burlington Glass Works, c. 1900.*

On the right is a pressed, flint-glass Beaded Oval and Fan *wine.* Star *motif on base. Three-piece mould. Height 3⅝". Jefferson Glass Company, Toronto, Ontario, c. 1925.*

169

168

170

FIGURE 171 *This array of pieces is decorated in the* Filly *or* Bull's Eye *pattern, all from Burlington Glass Works, Hamilton, Ontario, c. 1895.*

Left to right: tumbler (height 3¾"); three-mould goblet (height 5"); three-mould wine (height 3⁹/₁₆"); three-mould goblet (height 5¾"); lamp (height 5½").

The lamp was made from a goblet. The technique consisted of reheating the upper edge of the goblet and hand manipulating it to a form that could accommodate a threaded brass collar. These pieces are not plentiful. See Canadian Glass c. 1825-1925, *p. 52.*

171

FIGURE 172 *The pressed, flint-glass tumbler on the left is decorated in the* Block *motif. Petal and flower etched on the rim. Height is 3¾".*

The Pillar *pattern decorates the tumbler second from left. Four-piece mould. Height 3¾". Trenton, Nova Scotia, c. 1890.*

In the centre is a pressed, flint-glass tumbler in the Burlington Dominion *motif. Height 3¾". Shards excavated on the site of the Burlington Glass Works, Hamilton, Ontario. Circa 1890.*

Second from right is a four-mould tumbler in the Late Nugget *pattern. Height 3⅞". Jefferson and Dominion Glass Company, Toronto, Montreal and elsewhere, c. 1920.*

On the far right is an example of the Early Nugget *pattern. Four-piece mould. Height 3¾". Sydenham Glass Company, Wallaceburg, Ontario, c. 1895.*

FIGURE 173 *These pressed, flint-glass tumblers have been inverted to reveal the motifs on the bases.*

On the left is a horseshoe with large star. Height 3½". Dominion Glass Company, Toronto, Ontario, c. 1925.

In the centre background is an example with a horseshoe on the base. Height 3". Dominion Glass Company, c. 1925.

In the centre foreground is a piece with fine ribbing and a portrait of Sir Wilfred Laurier. Height 3⅞". Diamond Glass Company, Montreal, P.Q., c. 1890.

The tumbler on the right has a horseshoe and small star. Height 3⅞". Dominion Glass Company, c. 1925.

FIGURE 174 *These three examples of two-mould pressed flint-glass pieces bear the tell-tale ring that indicates they were sold as containers for mustard, peanut butter, etc. When the contents were removed, the container became a mug. They were produced by Jefferson Glass Company, Toronto, Montreal, etc. c. 1920-25. The two pieces on the left are in the St. Louis pattern. Heights (left to right) 5⅛", 4⅞", 4⅜".*

174

FIGURE 175 *On the left is a blown in the mould flint-glass tumbler decorated with a rendition of Wolfe and Montcalm. Height 3¹³/₁₆"; diameter 2¾". Quebec, c. 1908.*

The tumbler second from left was also blown in the mould. Decorated with Greek key, fleurs-de-lis and banded patterns. Height 3¾"; diameter 3".

The flint-glass tumbler second from right has been acid-etched with the decoration on the interior. Motifs include fleurs-de-lis, stars and geometrics. Dominion Glass Company, Montreal, P.Q., c. 1915.

On the far right is a clear, flint-glass tumbler blown in the mould. Decorated with a rendition of the Lord's Prayer, as well as two angels. Height 3¾"; diameter 2½".

173

FIGURE 176 *The two tumblers on the left have been blown, the two on the right pressed.*

On the far left is a clear, flint-glass tumbler decorated with moulded geese and bullrushes (height 4½", diameter 2⅞"). Beside it is a tumbler with a reproduction of the Canadian three-pence postage stamp created for the centennial of the Dominion Glass Company.

Second from the right is a pressed, flint-glass container with a Picket Fence motif (height 3"). Such containers were filled with cheese, etc., and closed with a metal cap. Dominion Glass Company, Montreal and elsewhere, c. 1925.

On the far right is a pressed, flint-glass tumbler with the base fluted in elongated blocks. Height 4½"; diameter at lip 3"; diameter at base 3½".

175

FIGURE 177 *The* Cross *pattern decorates these pieces. Creamer: height 4½". Covered sugar: height 6¼". See* Canadian Glass c. 1825-1925, *p. 214. The vinegar cruet was pressed ''upside down'' and is a very early example of this technique. The stopper is original which greatly increases the importance of the cruet. Overall height 6". Burlington Glass Works, Hamilton, Ontario, c. 1900.*

FIGURE 178 *The covered sugar, creamer, spooner and covered, footed bowl are all in the* Late Nugget *motif. Sugar: height 6½". Creamer: height 4½". Spooner: height 4½". Bowl height: 11½"; diameter 8½".*

The footed jug on the far right is in the Early Nugget *pattern. Height 8"; diameter, lip to handle, 7½". See* In a Canadian Attic, *p. 141.*

177

178

FIGURE 179 *These pieces illustrate the newly identified* Hedlin Shell *pattern (see Ch. 5). They were made at the Burlington Glass Works, Hamilton, Ontario, c. 1890.*

The nappy on the left has a shell handle (height 1³/₄"; diameter, including handle, 4¹/₈"). The footed nappy in the centre background has a shell motif on the handles (height 2¹/₄"; diameter 4"). In the centre foreground is a butter pat (length 3¹/₄"). The footed nappy on the right was made in a four-piece mould (height 1³/₄").

FIGURE 180 *The* Colonial *motif decorates this pressed, flint-glass, two-piece bowl. Bowl and stand pressed in four-piece moulds. Overall height 11"; diameter of bowl 15". Jefferson Glass Company, Toronto, Montreal and elsewhere in Canada,* c. *1913.*

FIGURE 181 *Three more examples of the* Colonial *pattern. Foted and covered bowl: height 11³/4"; diameter 8". Nappy: height 1¹/2"; diameter 3⁷/8". Footed bowl: height 5¹/2"; diameter 8¹/4". Jefferson Glass Company, Toronto, Montreal and elsewhere,* c. *1913. See* Canadian Glass c. *1825-1925, pps. 164-167.*

180

181

FIGURE 182 *Pressed, two-mould flint-glass wash basin and pitcher sets in this size with a* Colonial *motif are rare. Both have* Rayed *bases. The height of the basin is 4⁵/₈", diameter 15¹/₂". The footed pitcher has a hand-worked lip and upper area. Height at lip 11"; diameter, including handle and lip, 11". Jefferson Glass Company, Toronto, Montreal and elsewhere in Canada,* c. *1913.*

182

FIGURE 183 *A group of salts. The piece on the left, in the* Colonial *pattern, was made at the Burlington Glass Works, Hamilton, Ontario; height 2½". The master salt shown second from left was made to look like a miniature compote; see* Early Canadian Glass, *p. 60.*

The two pieces on the right were pressed in two-piece moulds. Height (second from right) 2³/₈". Height of the Colonial *variant on the right 1³/₄". Both from the Jefferson Glass Company, Toronto, Montreal and elsewhere in Canada, c. 1925.*

FIGURE 184 *These dishes and bowls are in the* Colonial *pattern. For reference, the celery on the right measures 7³/₄" high; diameter 4½". The footed bowl on the far right measures 7" high, diameter 8½". Jefferson Glass Company, Toronto, Montreal and elsewhere, c. 1913.*

FIGURE 185 *The* Colonial *pattern appeared in many shapes and sizes. Footed bowl with handles: height at handles 4¹/₈"; diameter at handles 5³/₄"; diameter at bowl 3½". Covered jar (centre background): height 6³/₄"; diameter 3". Covered butter tub (centre foreground): height 4½", diameter 4½". Jefferson Glass Company, Toronto, Montreal and elsewhere.*

183

184

18

FIGURE 186 *Tea service pieces in the* Horseshoe *motif, all with* Rayed *bases. The pressed, flint-glass, covered sugar on the left was made in a four-piece mould and is beaded on the connecting edge of the lid (overall height 6¹/₂", diameter 3³/₄"). The covered butter dish has a fluted edge; four-piece mould (height 5³/₄", diameter 7⁵/₈"). The upper edge of the spooner has been hand-worked; four-piece mould (height 4¹/₂"). Jefferson Glass Company, Toronto, Ontario, c. 1920.*

186

FIGURE 187 *Three examples of the* Horsehoe *pattern. The bowl on the left measures 3¹/₂" high, diameter 8⁷/₈". The nappy beside it is 1³/₄" high and 4¹/₄" in diameter. The tumbler has a* Rayed *base; four-piece mould; height 4". See* Canadian Glass c. 1825-1925, p. 188. *Jefferson Glass Company, Toronto, Ontario, c. 1920.*

187

FIGURE 188 *The pressed, flint-glass egg cup on the left is in the* Colonial *pattern. Two-piece mould. Height 4½". Jefferson Glass Company, Toronto, Ontario, c. 1925.*

In the centre is a pressed, flint-glass toothpick holder. Two piece mould. Six fleurs-de-lis, *serrated edges.* Rayed *base. Not a common item. Height 2½". Burlington Glass Works, Hamilton, Ontario, c. 1900.*

The pressed, flint-glass egg cup on the right was made in a two-piece mould. Wheel-engraved with Fern *motifs. Jefferson Glass Company, Toronto, c. 1925.*

188

FIGURE 189 *This group of six nappies contains examples of patterns found elsewhere in this chapter.*

On the left is a handled piece in the Panelled Forget-Me-Not *pattern. Height 1½".*

Above and to the right of it is a nappy in the Daisy and X-Band *design with scalloped edges. Height 2¾"; diameter 5½". See* Canadian Glass, c. 1825-1925, *p. 174.*

The piece below and to the right of it illustrates the Palmette *motif. Height 1"; diameter 3¼".*

Second from left in the foreground shows the Nova Scotia Beaded Grape *pattern. Height 1½". See* Early Canadian Glass, *p. 68.*

Third from left in the foreground is a footed nappy decorated with the Canadian *pattern. Height 2½"; diameter 3½".*

The piece below and to the left of it illustrates the Palmette *motif. Height 1"; diameter 3¼".*

189

FIGURE 190 *A covered butter dish (height 5¹/₂", diameter 7¹/₂") and an open sugar (height 3¹/₂" in pattern #358 from the Jefferson Glass Company, Toronto, Montreal and elsewhere. See* Canadian Glass c. 1825-1925, *p. 193.*

FIGURE 191 *Four illustrations of the Saw-tooth pattern. Footed creamer: height 5". Footed spooner: height 5¹/₂". The celery was made in a three-piece mould, and the upper area and rim have been worked; height 9¹/₂". The covered sugar stands on a Rayed base; height, base to finial, 7¹/₂". Burlington Glass Works, Hamilton, Ontario, c. 1885. See* Canadian Glass c. 1825-1925, *p. 214.*

FIGURE 192 *The covered sugar shown here was illustrated in Figure 191 with its cover removed. The two footed, covered bowls are also decorated with the Sawtooth pattern. The cover, foot and bowl of the piece on the left were made in two-piece moulds; height 12¹/₈". The bowl on the right measures 10¹/₄" high; diameter 6³/₄". Burlington Glass Works, Hamilton, Ontario, c. 1890.*

191

190

192

FIGURE 193 *Three pieces in the* Dominion *pattern. On the left is a pressed, flint-glass, footed butter dish with cover. Cover and base pressed in three-piece moulds. Base slightly ribbed. Height 7¹/₄"; diameter at the widest 7¹/₂". See* Canadian Glass c. 1825-1925, *p. 213. The* Dominion *nappy in the centre measures 2⁵/₈" high; diameter 3¹/₂". On the right is a pressed, flint-glass, covered cheese dish. The cover has been etched with a floral band. Height 6¹/₂"; diameter 8¹/₂".*

FIGURE 194 *A lead-glass, footed salver in the* Sawtooth *motif. A very large and impressive piece. Height 6³/₄"; diameter 14¹/₄".*

193

194

FIGURE 195 *On the left is a footed fruit bowl with scalloped edges and foot with slight variations of the* Sawtooth *design. Height 7¹/2"; diameter 9". Burlington Glass Works, Hamilton, Ontario, c. 1890.*

In the centre is a footed bowl with the same pattern. Height 6"; diameter 7³/4".

On the right is a footed, mould-blown, flintglass water pitcher in the Sawtooth *motif.*

This excellent example from the Burlington Glass Works illustrates their preference for fine hand work, rather than the use of the ever available pressing moulds. The neck, lip and upper area were hand-worked, and the graceful handle with slight trailing was applied. Height to top of handle 9¹/8". Made Circa 1885.

195

FIGURE 196 *Three pieces in the* Six-Point Star
*(#279) pattern, but in a variant style. Left to
right: tumbler; covered bon-bon dish (height
7¹/₂", diameter 4³/₄"); sugar (cover missing). All
were made by the Jefferson Glass Company,
Toronto, Montreal and elsewhere. See* Canadian Glass c. 1825-1925.

196

FIGURE 197 *Each of these examples has a cover, finial and bowl decorated with the* Dominion *pattern. The pressed, flint-glass sugar bowl on the left has a cover and base pressed in three-piece moulds. Height 9". Burlington Glass Works, Hamilton, Ontario, and elsewhere,* c. *1890.*

The pressed, flint-glass, footed bowl with cover on the right measures 11½" high; diameter 8".

197

FIGURE 198 *Pressed, flint-glass slipper and dressing table jar, both decorated with* Nova Scotia Diamond *motifs. An interesting aspect of the slipper is that it is mounted on a sled which, in turn, is decorated with snowshoes —a very Canadian design. Trenton, Nova Scotia, c. 1890.*

FIGURE 199 *The* Dominion *motif also decorates these jars. The pattern shows on the neck and lid of the apothecary (candy) jar on the left. Base cut with starburst. Clear body. Height 11½"; diameter 4¾".*

On the right is a pressed, flint-glass, circular candy jar; footed. Base, lip and stopper patterned. Height 9½"; diameter 4".

198

199

FIGURE 200 Nova Scotia Diamond *is the motif on the bowl on the left, further decorated with wheel-engraved* Flower and Star. *Height 2¾"; diameter 7½". See George MacLaren's* Nova Scotia Glass *and* Canadian Glass c. 1825-1925, *p. 215.*

The footed dish with handle is in the Dominion *pattern. Vertical angled edge (1¼") and clear lip (1"). Height 6¼", diameter 9½".*

200

FIGURE 201 *Two jugs in the* Nova Scotia Star Flower *pattern. Left: height 7¹/4"; diameter 4¹/2". Right: height 8¹/4"; diameter 8".*

FIGURE 202 *The covered sugar (height 7¹/4"), spooner (height 4¹/2") and the creamer (height 6") form a set in the* Nova Scotia Star Flower *pattern. See MacLaren's* Nova Scotia Glass.

The bowl is a footed Pillar *variant of the* Nova Scotia Diamond Ray *design. Height 6¹/2"; diameter 8". See* Nova Scotia Glass.

FIGURE 203 *Three more examples of the* Nova Scotia Star Flower *pattern. On the left is a footed bowl (height 6¹/4", diameter 8"). In the centre is a footed cake salver. On the right is a footed bowl with cover (height 10", diameter 7").*

201

202

20

FIGURE 204 *Two spooner and creamer sets. On the left is the* Bead and Petal *design (spooner height 4¹/2". creamer height 4¹/2"). Nova Scotia. See* Canadian Glass c. 1825-1925, *p. 113. On the right is the* Nova Scotia Floral *pattern (spooner height 5", creamer height 5³/4"). See* Nova Scotia Glass, *George MacLaren, p. 27.*

FIGURE 205 *The* Pillar *motif decorates these three pieces. The celery, oddly enough, is a very rare form in this pattern. It is on the left and measures 5³/4" high, diameter 4¹/8". The bon-bon dish is 2¹/4" high, length (tip to tip) 8¹/2", width 4". The cake salver was made in a four-piece mould (height 6¹/2", diameter 10¹/2"). See* Nova Scotia Glass, *p. 37. Lamont Glass Company, Trenton, Nova Scotia, c. 1890.*

FIGURE 206 *Additional examples of the* Pillar *pattern, all of which were made in four-piece moulds. The honey pot with cover on the left is 4¹/2" high. The covered relish dish in the centre is 6⁷/8" high. And the covered marmalade jar on the right is 5" high. Because the casualty rate of tops on covered glass dishes or stoppered cruets is very high, collectors should be particularly interested in pieces with original tops. Always examine open pots, compotes and the like for any evidence indicating they once had covers. Lamont Glass Company, Trenton, Nova Scotia, c. 1890.*

205

204

FIGURE 207 *A four-piece table setting in the* Pillar *pattern manu-factured in four-piece moulds. Fern engraving. Left to right: covered sugar (height 4¼", diameter 4½"); creamer (height 3⅞", diameter 3½"); covered butter dish (height to finial 5½", diameter 6⅛"); spooner (height 3⅝", diameter 4"). Lamont Glass Company, Trenton, Nova Scotia,* c. *1890.*

FIGURE 208 *The pressed, flint-glass* Pillar *cheese dish and cover were made in four-piece moulds. The bell and finial decorated with the* Pillar *motif, while in the base a large central star is out-lined in a* Sawtooth *pattern. Height 7⅛", diameter 9⅛".*

The pressed, flint-glass, Pillar *water jug was made in a four-piece mould. Water jugs in this pattern are very rare and highly collectible. Applied handle. Height to lip 8".*

Both pieces are from the Lamont Glass Company, Trenton, Nova Scotia, c. *1890.*

FIGURE 209 *A group of pieces in the* Pillar *pattern from the Lamont Glass Company, Trenton, Nova Scotia,* c. *1890.* Pillar *is one of the more collectible and attractive of the pressed glass patterns.*

The footed bowl with fluted lip on the left measures 7½" high and 8" in diameter. In the centre background is a footed bowl with cover; four-piece mould; height 11⅝". The plate in the foreground is nearly square (7¼" × 7¼"). The footed bowl on the right has a fused lip (height 8½", diameter 9½").

208

207

209

FIGURE 210 Nova Scotia Dahlia. *The pressed, flint-glass, oval dish on the left was made in a two-piece mould. Scalloped edge. Height 2"; length 8⅝". Trenton, Nova Scotia, c. 1890.*

The group on the left constitutes a three-piece set. The tray was made in a two-piece mould (length 9¼", width 5⅝"). The pressed, flint-glass creamer was blown in a two-piece mould (height 3¼", width 5½"). *The pressed, flint-glass sugar also came from a two-piece mould (height 2¾", width 5¾"). Shards of this specific design were excavated at Trenton, Nova Scotia. These pieces should not be confused with the U.S. design of the same name.* Circa 1890.

210

FIGURE 211 *The footed bowl with cover on the left is* Nova Scotia Grape and Vine. *Height 9½"; diameter 6". See George MacLaren,* Nova Scotia Glass.

The pressed, flint-glass, footed bowl with cover on the right is also Grape and Vine. *The cover is decorated with* Grape and Vine *and* Fine Rib *motifs. The finial is octagonal. Cover pressed in a three-piece mould; base in two-piece mould. Height 12". Trenton, Nova Scotia, c. 1890.*

211

FIGURE 212 *On the left is a covered cheese dish in the* Nova Scotia Grape and Vine *pattern. Height 8¼"; diameter 8".*

The pressed, flint-glass plate in the centre is decorated with a Diamond *motif on the base,* Grape and Vine *on lower edge and* Fine Rib *on rim. Diameter 10⅞". Trenton, Nova Scotia, c. 1890.*

Nova Scotia Ribbed Band is the pattern that decorates the creamer on the right. Height 5½". See MacLaren's Nova Scotia Glass.

212

FIGURE 213 *Shown here is a rare, pressed, flint-glass, footed bowl and cover in the* Nova Scotia Ribbon and Star *pattern. Height 12¹/₂"; diameter of bowl 8⁵/₈". Trenton, Nova Scotia, c. 1890.*

FIGURE 214 *The* Nova Scotia Ribbon and Star *decorates the celery and bowl shown here. Celery height 6"; diameter 4¹/₄". Bowl: height 4"; diameter 8¹/₂". See MacLaren's* Nova Scotia Glass, *p. 12.*

FIGURE 215 *Two examples of a* Nova Scotia Ribbon and Star *variant pattern. Left: height 3"; diameter 9". Right: height 2¹/₂"; diameter 9³/₄". Trenton, Nova Scotia, c. 1890. See MacLaren, p. 81.*

213

214

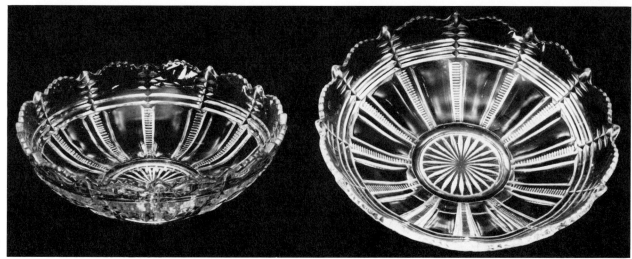

215

FIGURE 216 *The footed bowl on the left is decorated in the* Nova Scotia Bow Tie *motif. Fluted and scalloped. Height 7³/4"; diameter 8¹/2".*

The footed bowl on the right is in the Early Nugget *pattern. Height 7¹/2"; diameter 8¹/2".*

In the foreground is a pressed, flint-glass plate, "No. 358 Ware." See Canadian Glass *c. 1825-1925, p. 184. Made in a four-piece mould. Diameter 11³/4". Jefferson Glass Company, Toronto, Ontario, c. 1920.*

216

FIGURE 217 *These four pieces illustrate the* Nova Scotia Bow Tie *pattern. Covered sugar: height 6". Creamer: height 3⅞". Jug: height 9"; diameter, handle to lip, 7½". Round bowl: height 3½", diameter 8".*

217

FIGURE 218 *The cake salver in the centre is in the* Beaded Grape *motif. Height 5½"; width 8½".*

The nappies in the foreground are (left to right); Bow Tie *(height 2¾", diameter 4"), see* Canadian Glass c. 1825-1925, *p. 176;* Woodrow; Nova Scotia Star Flower *(height 1", diameter 4⅛");* and Beaded Oval and Fan No. 1.

FIGURE 219 *On the left is a creamer in the* Tassel and Crest *pattern (height 5½"). On the right is a covered and footed bowl in the same motif (height 10½", diameter 6¾"). See George Mac-Laren's* Nova Scotia Glass, *p. 28.*

FIGURE 220 *Two footed bowls decorated with the* Nova Scotia Panelled Forget-Me-Not *design. Left: height 8¼", diameter 8½". Right: height 7"; diameter 7¼". See* Canadian Glass c. 1825-1925, *p. 216.*

218

FIGURE 221 *Additional illustrations of the* Nova Scotia Panelled Forget-Me-Not *pattern. The footed bowl measures 6¹/₂" high; diameter 8". The footed spooner, covered sugar and creamer form a set. Spooner: height 5". Sugar: height 6³/₄". Creamer: height 5¹/₂".*

221

FIGURE 222 *A group of pieces in the pattern known as* Beaded Oval and Fan No. 1. *The covered butter dish in the foreground measures 5³/₄″ high. Left to right: spooner (height 5″), covered sugar (height 7³/₄″), creamer (height 5¹/₂″).*

222

FIGURE 223 *The footed cake salver on the left is decorated with the* Beaded Oval and Fan No. 1 *motif (height 5", diameter 9¼").* *The jug in the foreground illustrates the* Canadian Drape *pattern (height 8¼"); see* Canadian Glass c. 1825-1925, *p. 222.* *The footed bowl on the right is in the* New York *pattern with the foot in the* Sawtooth *design (height 7½", diameter 7¾").*

223

FIGURE 224 *The* Beaded Band *motif decorates these pieces. In the centre is a blown, three-mould syrup pitcher in flint glass. Applied, pressed-glass handle and metal top. Height 6¼". Authenticated by shards excavated at the site of the Burlington Glass Works, Hamilton, Ontario. Made* circa *1885.*

The footed bowl with cover on the right measures 9¼" high; diameter 6". See Canadian Glass c. 1825-1925, *p. 216.*

224

FIGURE 225 *A flint-glass water pitcher in the* Daisy and Button *motif. Footed base and bottom decorated with a* Rayed *design. The upper area was reheated and worked to form a graceful edge and lip; wheel-engraved with a semi-circular floral design. Applied handle. Height at handle 9¹/₄"; diameter, handle to lip, 8³/₈". Burlington Glass Works, Hamilton, Ontario,* c. *1890.*

FIGURE 226 *The pressed, flint-glass vinegar cruet was pressed "upside down" and decorated with the* Daisy and Button *motif. Height 5¹/₂". Burlington Glass Works, Hamilton, Ontario,* c. *1900.*

The pressed, flint-glass inkwell is in the Nova Scotia Diamond *pattern. Four-piece mould. Height 2⁷/₈"; diameter at base 3³/₈". Trenton, Nova Scotia,* c. *1890.*

225

226

FIGURE 227 *A pressed, lead-glass, footed bowl in the* New York (Honeycomb) *pattern. Pressed, lead-glass base also associated with the* Sawtooth *motif. Height 10¹⁄₈"; diameter 11⁵⁄₈". A very impressive piece of Canadian glass. Burlington Glass Works, Hamilton, Ontario, c. 1895.*

227

FIGURE 228 *The* Stippled Swirl and Star *motif is seen on these examples. Left to right: covered sugar (height 7¹/2"); spooner (height 4³/4"); footed plate (height 5¹/2", diameter 9¹/2"). See* Canadian Glass c. 1825-1925, *p. 124.*

FIGURE 229 *Each of the pieces pictured here is decorated in the* Block *motif.*

In the background is a pressed, clear-glass cake salver turned on edge to show the pattern. Height 5⁵/8"; diameter 9".

The pressed, flint-glass rose bowl on the left has a Rayed *base that has been ground. The upper edge has been reheated and the opening reduced in size. Height 4". Burlington Glass Works, Hamilton, Ontario, c. 1890.*

Beside the bowl is an open jam pot (height 2⁷/8"), while second from right is a creamer

(height to lip 3¹/2"). The covered sugar on the right measures 6¹/2" high. See Canadian Glass c. 1825-1925, *p. 214.*

FIGURE 230 *Three pieces in the* 101 *pattern. The creamer on the left measures 4¹/2" high. The foot and upper area of the jug (height 9³/4") were pressed in three-piece moulds, and the rim, lip and upper area were hand-worked. The jug's trailed handle was applied. The pressed, flint-glass celery (height 8¹/8") was made in a three-piece mould, and the upper area was hand-worked and finished with a serrated rim. All were made at the Burlington Glass Works, Hamilton, Ontario, c. 1885. See* Canadian Glass c. 1825-1925, *p. 223.*

229

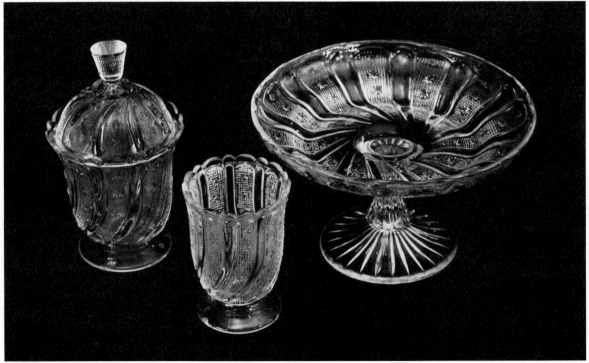

228

23

FIGURE 231 *The* Athenian *motif decorates these pieces. The covered butter dish in the centre foreground measures 5" high, diameter 7¼". From left to right in the background: covered creamer (height 6½"), covered sugar (height 8"), spooner (height 4½"). See* Canadian Glass c. 1825-1925, *p. 125.*

231

FIGURE 232 *The pressed, flint-glass, footed creamer on the left is in the* Palmette *motif. Three-piece mould. The upper area and lip have been hand worked. The handle has slight trailing and was hand applied. Height 6³/₈".*
Also in Palmette *is the blown, three-mould syrup pitcher of flint glass. Rayed base, applied handle, metal top. Height 7".*

To the right is a Palmette, *pressed, flint-glass, footed celery. The rim was hand-worked to create a gently serrated design. Height 8³/₈".*
All of the pieces shown here were made at the Burlington Glass Works, Hamilton, Ontario, c. 1885.

FIGURE 233 *Additional illustrations of the* Palmette *pattern. In the centre is a flint-glass, footed bowl with cover (overall height 11¾"). Foot, bowl and cover pressed in two-piece moulds. The creamer, spooner and each of the pieces in the cruet set carry the same motifs. The dish in the centre foreground is avocado-shaped (length 8½", width 4¾"). Burlington Glass Works, Hamilton, Ontario, c. 1885. See* Canadian Glass c. 1825-1925, *p. 214.*

233

FIGURE 234 *The* Daisy and X-Band *pattern. The spooner on the left measures 5½" high. The footed bowl in the centre measures 4" high to the scalloped edge. The sugar on the right (cover missing) is 4" high. In the foreground, on the left, is a footed bowl (height 2", diameter 5¼"). The footed nappy in the right foreground is 2¼" high, diameter 3¼".*

FIGURE 235 *The plate, wine and goblet shown here demonstrate additional forms of the* Daisy and X-Band *pattern. The goblet, in particular, has become rare and, surprisingly, seems to be one of the more difficult to find to complete a collection.*

234

235

FIGURE 236 *Three illustrations of the* Thistle *pattern produced by the Jefferson Glass Company, Toronto, Ontario* c. *1915-1925. This pattern was also made in the United States. U.S. Higby Glass examples are most frequently found and can be identified by a stylized bee pressed on the bottom, ordinarily inside. Both the goblet and wine were made in three-piece moulds (heights 5⅜″, 3⅝″). The plate was pressed in a four-piece mould (width 10⅞″).*

FIGURE 237 *A close-up of the* Thistle *pattern made by the Jefferson Glass Company, Toronto, Ontario,* c. *1915-1925.*

237

236

FIGURE 238 *The* Thistle *pattern footed bowl in the centre measures 7" high, diameter 8". The nappy on the left is 2" high, diameter 4¹/2". The ''upside down'' pressed, flint-glass vinegar cruet is 4¹/2" high. Jefferson Glass Company, Toronto, Ontario, c. 1915.*

238

FIGURE 239 *These pieces are decorated in the* Canadian *motif which includes vignettes illustrating mountains, lakes, rural scenes, buildings, ships, rocky cliffs, etc. Numerous shards of this pattern were unearthed at the site of the Burlington Glass Works, Hamilton, Ontario. The examples shown here were made* circa *1880-1890.*

The goblet and wine were pressed in three-piece moulds. Heights 6¹/₄″, 4¹/₈″.

The two plates also employ maple leaves along the borders. Widths, including handles, 12″, 9¹/₂″.

FIGURE 240 *Examples of the* Canadian *pattern. On the left is a footed bowl (height 7″, diameter 8″). In the centre is a footed bowl (height 5¹/₄″, diameter 8″). The height of the covered, footed bowl on the right is 9¹/₄″. Burlington Glass Works, Hamilton, Ontario,* c. *1885.*

FIGURE 241 *A set in the* Canadian *design. The footed creamer (height 6″) is decorated with three "views;" note the foot, handle and floral motifs. The footed butter dish measures 6″ high. There are nine possible vignettes in this pattern, and there are no duplications. Burlington Glass Works, Hamilton, Ontario,* c. *1885.*

241

FIGURE 242 *The* Maple Leaf *design decorates three of these pieces. On the left is a cake salver (height 4³/4", diameter 10") turned on edge to show the pattern. The jug beside it measures 6¹/2" high; diameter 7¹/4". The footed bowl is 7¹/4" high and 7¹/2" in diameter.*

In the foreground is a pressed, flint-glass plate with ten maple leaves on the rim and the Arms of Montreal in its centre. Diameter 10¹/2". The (early) Dominion Glass Company, Montreal, P.Q., c. 1895.

FIGURE 243 *An illustration of the various types of pieces made in the* Maple Leaf *pattern, including a footed bowl, spooner, covered sugar, creamer and plate.*

243

FIGURE 244 *A four-piece table setting in the* Rayed Heart *pattern: creamer, covered sugar, spooner and covered butter dish.*

FIGURE 245 *The bowl in the centre of this photograph (height 3¼", diameter 8") bears the* Rayed Heart *motif. Grouped around it are nappies. Left to right, counter clockwise:* Maple Leaf *(height 1½", diameter 4⅛");* Athenian *(height 1½", diameter 4");* Rayed Heart *(height 1⅞", diameter 4");* Beaded Oval and Fan No. 1 *(height 1½", diameter 4"); and* Late Nugget *(height 1⅝", diameter 4¼").*

For further references to these pieces, see Canadian Glass c. 1825-1925. *pps. 175, 177-78, and* In a Canadian Attic, *p. 141.*

244

245

FIGURE 246 *Two illustrations of the* Leaf and Dart *pattern. The mould-blown, flint-glass, footed water pitcher was pressed in a three-piece mould. The upper area and lip were hand-worked. The trailed handle was applied. Height at handle 9". Burlington Glass Works, Hamilton, Ontario, c. 1885.*

The pressed, flint-glass, footed creamer also has a hand worked lip and upper area. It was made at the same site but circa 1890.

246

FIGURE 247 *The* Woodrow *pattern was produced in Canada between about 1900 and 1925. The design is documented in a catalogue issued by the Jefferson Glass Company. The trade number for the pattern was 1501.*

In the upper left of this photograph is an interesting example of both the design and glass-making technique. This flint-glass syrup jug appears to have been mould-blown. However, a study of the exterior base does not reveal a ground or rough pontil mark, but it does show a very small, swirled indentation, which indicates that the object was pressed *"upside down." The result was a wide open base that was closed by twisting the excess, still workable glass in a manner which closed the opening. The miniature swirl left provides proof of a not-too-well-known technique.*

The flint-glass vinegar cruet in the centre was produced in the same manner in about 1925. Height 6⅞".

FIGURE 248 *This and the following nine illustrations feature the* Woodrow *pattern made by the Jefferson (Dominion) Glass Company, Toronto, Ontario.*

On the left is a tumbler that has been heightened with gold flashing. Rayed base. Three-piece mould. Height 3⁵⁄₆". Circa 1925.

Beside the tumbler (left to right) are a bowl, nappy and creamer.

FIGURE 249 *A four-piece* Woodrow *table setting.*

FIGURE 250 *Four pieces showing the range of pieces available in the* Woodrow *design.*

248

249

250

247

FIGURE 251 *The flint-glass,* Woodrow *water carafe on the left was pressed "upside down." Height 9¹/₈". Jefferson Glass Company, Toronto, c. 1915.*

The wine in the centre of the photograph was made in a three-piece mould. Height 4¹/₄". Circa 1925.

The Woodrow *goblet on the right was heightened with gold flashing. Three-piece mould. Height 6". Circa 1915.*

FIGURE 252 *Four additional illustrations of the* Woodrow *pattern made by the Jefferson Glass Company, Toronto, Ontario, c. 1900-1925.*

FIGURE 253 *Three pieces in the* Woodrow *design.*

FIGURE 254 *The* Woodrow *pattern.*

251

FIGURE 255 *The pressed, flint-glass basket on the left was made when a* Woodrow *motif celery was reheated and the upper area given the basket form and applied handle. Rare. Overall height 12¾". Made circa 1915.*

The basket on the right was made in a similar manner but using a tumbler of the Colonial *pattern. Height 7¼". Jefferson Glass Company, Toronto, Ontario, c. 1915.*

FIGURE 256 *Three pressed and hand-worked ''swung'' vases. ''Swung'' vases were quite popular and were produced in several colours and motifs. The technique consisted of pressing a vase, and then by use of a clamp ''swinging'' the piece in such a manner that the upper portion became elongated. These examples were made* circa 1925.

255

256

FIGURE 257 *On the left is a mould-blown, flint-glass syrup jug. Two-piece mould. Wheel-engraved floral motifs. The handle was applied with one trailing end; upon it is a "turkey track" mark indicating the use of a tool that was employed in* many *glass factories in Canada and the United States. The mark should not be used as authentication to a specific source. This piece was made in Hamilton, or St. Johns, P.Q., or Montreal,* c. *1885.*

The syrup jug on the right, however, was definitely pressed in a two-piece mould at the Burlington Glass Works, c. *1900.*

FIGURE 258 *A pressed candlestick made by the Jefferson Glass Company, Toronto, Ontario,* c. *1913-1925. See* Canadian Glass c. *1825-1925, p. 196.*

257

258

FIGURE 259 *On the left is a pressed, flint-glass pitcher made in a two-piece mould. Motifs include ''Pints,'' ''Pounds'' and a ''Chinese'' figure. Legend on base, ''Ocean Mills, Montreal, Canada.'' Height 8¼". Dominion Glass, Montreal, P.Q., c. 1930.*

On the right is a similar jug with flying wild duck motifs. Height 9½". Dominion Glass, c. 1930.

259

FIGURE 260 *A group of three commercial containers. The piece on the left is from the Dominion Glass Company, marked "W. H. Donovan Reg'd Halifax." The amber, quart-sized milk bottle on the right is imprinted "Not to be bought or sold" and was made in the Hamilton Glass Works. The bottle in the foreground is marked "JNO Verner Beaver Trademark Toronto."*

FIGURE 261 *On the left is a commercial container decorated with maple leaves and made by the Dominion Glass Company. In the centre is a piece excavated on the site of the Manitoba Glass Manufacturing Company, Beausejour, Manitoba, which was active from 1907 to 1914. The printing on it reads: "E L Brewery Winnipeg. This bottle is our property. Any charge made therefore simply covers its use while containing goods bottled by us and must be returned when empty." On the right is a preserving jar made by the Hamilton Glass Works.*

260

261

FIGURE 262 *Left to right: Dominion Soda Water Mfg. Co., deer trademark, Hamilton, Ontario. Eamer & Cameron, dove trademark, Cornwall, Ontario. Green Vess Dry bottle, "Patented," 6½ fl. ozs.*

FIGURE 263 *On the left and in the centre are two "Warranted" flasks. On the right is a "Shoofly Flask," marked "#4" on the bottom. All three are made of pressed glass and manufactured by the Dominion Glass Company Limited.*

FIGURE 264 *The Dominion Glass Company manufactured these commercial containers. Left to right: amber Crown, aquamarine Crown ("Imperial Qt.") and an aquamarine Beaver jar.*

263

264

FIGURE 265 *A set of three pieces in opal glass. The pattern includes decorations in the form of shells,* fleurs-de-lis, *and vines and flowers. Finials have crown motifs. The covered jam jar on the left measures 5½" high. The covered sugar in the centre is 5" high. The covered creamer on the right has ''No. 1'' on the base and measures 5" high.*

This design in opal glass was authenticated as Canadian by shards found at the site of the Burlington Glass Works, Hamilton, Ontario. The set was made circa 1890.

FIGURE 266 *Shown here is a four-piece, white opal glass table setting in the* Maple Leaf *pattern. Montreal, Toronto, Hamilton, Wallaceburg, c. 1890-1915.*

The base of the pressed butter dish on the left is decorated on the underside with sixteen maple leaves and a Rayed *motif (diameter 7³/₈"). The cover is decorated with five large leaves on the dome and one on the knob finial (diameter 5¹/₁₆").*

The spooner has five maple leaves and a Rayed *base. Three-piece mould. Height 4".*

The covered sugar second from right has a bowl with six maple leaves and a base with a Rayed *motif (height 4"). The cover is decorated with eight leaves, and the finial with four (height 2⁵/₈").*

The creamer on the right has six leaves and a Rayed *base. Three-piece mould. Height 4".*

265

FIGURE 267 *On the left is a white opal cheese pot. Height 4½". Burlington Glass Works, Hamilton, Ontario.*

Second from left is a pressed, opal vigil light (with ''D'' in base) and stand. Designs include ''Pray for Us'' over a sprig motif and a cross over a sprig. Overall height 3⁷/₁₆". Dominion Glass Company, Montreal, P.Q.

The pressed, white opal egg cup second from right was made in a two-piece mould and measures 4½" high. This specific design and colour were much admired by Burlington glass-workers, who reheated the upper area and created whimsey hats, etc. Burlington Glass Works, c. 1890.

On the right is a white opal cheese pot with the legend, ''MacLaren Imperial Cheese.'' Height 3¹/₄". Burlington.

266

FIGURE 268 *A pair of mould-blown, opal-glass cookie jars with original enamel decorations. The Britannia-metal lids carry the trademark of the Toronto Silver Plate Company which was active from 1882 through 1907. Height of bowls 6¹/₈"; circumferences 18". Burlington Glass Works, c. 1890. See* Canadian Glass c. 1825-1925, *p. 221.*

FIGURE 269 *On the left is a mould-blown, opal seed cup for a bird cage. Ribbed design with a central* Crown *motif. Height 3". Excavated complete at the site of the Burlington Glass Works, Hamilton, Ontario. Circa 1880.*

Second from left is a miniature oblong tray with a painted floral design in the centre.

Third from left is an opal glass container, "For Burnt Matches," blown in a two-piece mould. The legend and well designed fleurs-de-lis provide data relative to the use for which this item was produced and an example of a truly Canadian motif found on numerous examples of mould-blown and pressed glass. Burlington Glass Works, c. 1890.

On the far right is a pressed, opal-glass miniature (butter?) dish. Length 3⁷/₁₆". Excavated at the Burlington site. Circa 1895.

268

269

FIGURE 270 *A pressed opal dish in the form of a fish. The legend on the base reads .''Pat. June 1872.'' Length 9½". Shards (See Fig. 127) excavated on the site of the Burlington Glass Works, Hamilton, Ontario. Made* circa *1880.*

FIGURE 271 *Two pressed plates with* Fleur-de-Lis *motifs on the edges. A multiplicity of shards with this pattern have been excavated at the Burlington site, and this design is credited to this greatest of all Canadian glass factories. The piece on the left is in opal glass (diameter 7⅜"). The plate on the right is in satin-type glass (diameter 7⅜"). Both made* circa *1890.*

270

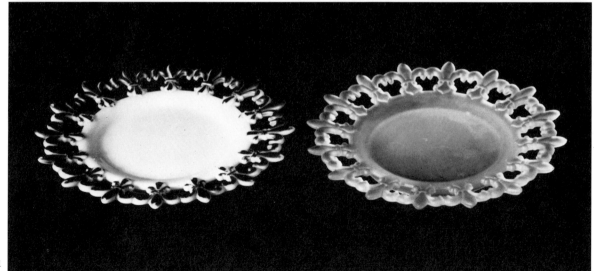

271

FIGURE 272 *A group of pressed, opal-glass square plates with open edges. The standing piece has vestiges of painted floral decorations (diameter 7⅛"). The example in the lower left has had the painted design removed. The two smaller plates on the right (one in blue opal and one in white) have vestiges of painted floral motifs. All four were made at the Burlington Glass Works, Hamilton, Ontario,* c. 1895.

FIGURE 273 *Three circular, pressed, opal plates with open edges. The painted rose design has been removed from the centre piece. Diameters 8⁵⁄₁₆". Authenticated by shards found at the site of the Burlington Glass Works, Hamilton, Ontario.* Circa 1895.

FIGURE 274 *Two pressed, opal-glass plates with* Club and Fan *motifs on the edges. The example on the left has the legend "Wilfred Laurier" and a portrait, both painted bronze, and a flag and maple leaves in colour (diameter 7⅜"). The piece on the right has the legend "Victoria R" and a portrait, both painted bronze (diameter 7⅛"). Burlington Glass Works, Hamilton, Ontario,* c. 1900.

FIGURE 275 *On the left is a pressed, opal "old oaken bucket" with metal bail handle made in a two-piece mould (height 2⁵⁄₈"). The pressed, "custard-glass" cream pitcher was made in a three-piece mould and with a* Horseshoe *motif and* Rayed *base (height 4¼"). Both from the Burlington Glass Works, Hamilton, Ontario,* c. 1900 *and* c. 1890.

273

274

272

275

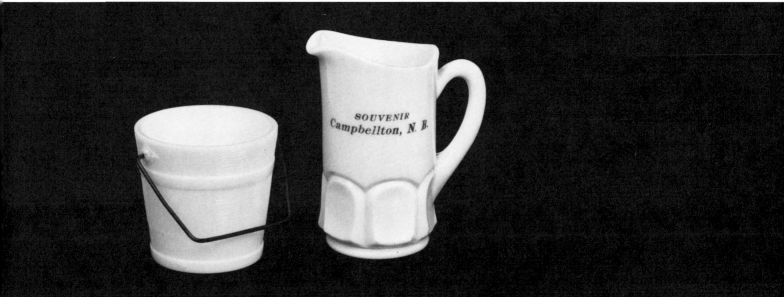

7

CUT GLASS

Canadian cut glass has been strangely neglected by the Canadian researcher and collector. Because much of it is signed, it is the easiest of the Canadian-made glass to authenticate. A great deal of excellent cutting was done in the first quarter of this century in Canada.

This short section does little more than recognize that this is a potentially exciting area. There is a great need for careful and exhaustive research and the publication of material on the factories, artists and designs.

We have collected a few pieces and will illustrate them here and record some of the signatures of the different factories, the production of which is important and collectable.

A section in my earlier book, *Canadian Glass c. 1825-1925*, is a limited but useful reference on Canadian cut glass.

FIGURE 276 *Gundy-Clapperton produced the pieces shown here. The celery dish measures 10⁷/₈" in length and 4⁷/₈" wide at the middle. The fruit bowl is 3¹/₂" high and 8¹/₂" wide.*

FIGURE 277 *Three tumblers from Gundy-Clapperton & Company, Deseronto, Ontario, c. 1905-1931. Each piece measures 3⁷/₈" high. The tumbler on the far right bears the* Tulip *design which was extensively used by Gundy-Clapperton. See* Canadian Glass c. 1825-1925, *pps. 235-41, and* Early Canadian Glass, *pps. 162-68. Gundy-Clapperton pieces are signed with the company's "three-leaf clover" containing the initials "G C Co."*

FIGURE 278 *These pieces are also from Gundy-Clapperton. The goblet on the left has the* Colonial *design (height 6¹/₄"). The goblet with the* Tulip *motif measures 6" high. The neck of the wine carafe has a serrated line design, while the bowl (circumference 20³/₄") bears the* Tulip *motif.*

277

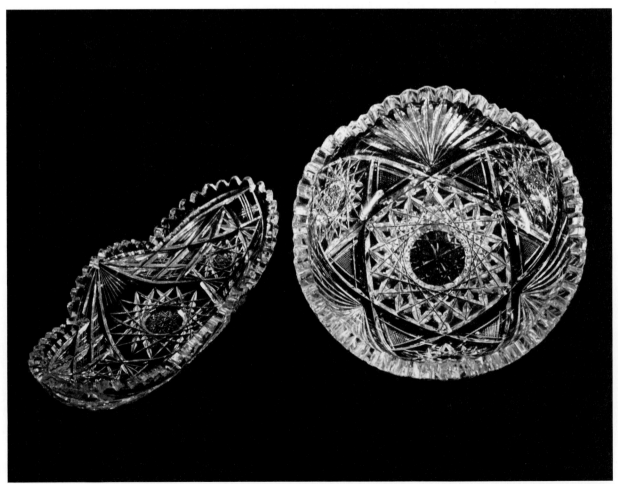

276

FIGURE 279 *The vase on the left is 8¹/8″ high. The open sugar with handles in the centre bears the Tulip motif (height 2⁷/8″, diameter 2⁷/8″). The rose bowl on the right also has the Tulip design (height 4¹/2″, circumference 17¹/2″, diameter of opening 3³/4″). All three are from Gundy-Clapperton & Company.*

279

FIGURE 280 *Great skill in cutting is exemplified in these two non-lead, flint-glass tumblers produced by craftsmen in the Excelsior Glass Works, Montreal, c. 1881. See* Canadian Glass, *p. 241.*

FIGURE 281 *This desk clock was produced by Gundy-Clapperton, Deseronto, Ontario. Height 5¼″.*

FIGURE 282 *In the foreground are a six-sided puff box and hair-receiver in the* Tulip *design (diameters 4½″). The dresser tray measures 14½″ long and 1″ deep. All three pieces are from Gundy-Clapperton.*

280

281

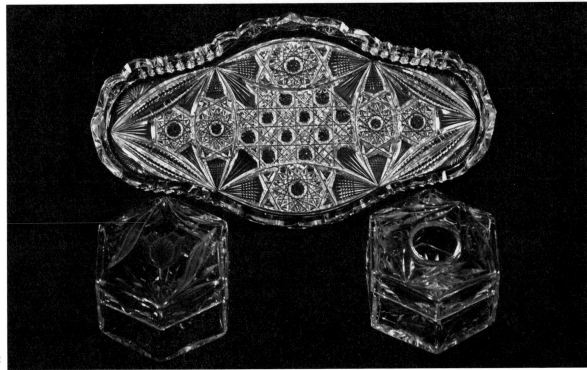

282

FIGURE 283 *The* Daisy *motif decorates the butter tub and fruit bowl shown here. The tub measures 1³/₄" high, 4⁷/₈" in diameter. The fruit bowl is 4¹/₂" high, 8⁷/₈" in diameter. Gundy-Clapperton & Company, Deseronto, Ontario,* c. *1905-1931.*

283

FIGURE 284 *Gowans, Kent & Co., Toronto, Ontario, produced these pieces in about 1900. The berry bowl on the left has a fluted edge; it measures 4" high, 7⁵/₁₆" in diameter. The matching nappy (one of a set of six) is 1³/₄" high and 4³/₈" in diameter. The height of the jug (to the lip) is 9¹/₂"; it is signed "Elite" in a maple leaf enclosed in a circle. See* Canadian Glass c. 1825-1925, *pps. 234-235.*

284

GLOSSARY

Blowpipe   A hollow iron rod, three to six feet long, with one tapered and one flared end. A gather of molten glass was taken from the batch on the flared end and shaped and manipulated by blowing into the tapered end.

Cullet   Glass salvaged from a previous melt; some cullet was added to each new batch.

Free Blown   Glass objects made without the use of moulds but employing in particular the blowpipe and pontil rod.

Gather   Molten glass taken from the batch on the "gathering" or flared end of the blowpipe.

Glory Hole   A small, movable furnace used for reheating, finishing and fire-polishing.

Lead Glass   "Crystal" glass made with oxide of lead.

Lime Glass   Non-lead glass with some brilliance but little resonance made with soda and lime as a flux. Also known as flint.

Metal   The term used by glassworkers to refer to finished or molten glass.

Mould Blown   Glass objects made in moulds the full size of the completed objects. Such objects may show pontil marks, but they always have seams corresponding to the sections of the particular mould; hence two-mould, three-mould, etc.

Pontil Rod (Punty)   A solid iron rod that the glassworker attached to the base of a glass object to allow the manipulation of it.

Pressed   Glass made in a mould operated by a pressman.

Pucellas   A U-shaped glassworker's tool made of iron.

Spring Tool   A U-shaped tool like the pucellas, but made by the house blacksmith to the requirements of the individual glassworker.

INDEX

Numbers given in ordinary type refer to pages, those that are italicized indicate plates.

BOOKS BY GERALD STEVENS

Old Stone House. Toronto: Ryerson Press, McGraw-Hill Company of Canada, 1954.

In a Canadian Attic. Toronto: The Ryerson Press, 1955.

The Canadian Collector. Toronto: The Ryerson Press, 1957.

Catalogue of the Edith Chown Pierce and Gerald Stevens Collection of Early Canadian Glass. Toronto: The Royal Ontario Museum, 1957.

Early Canadian Glass. Toronto: The Ryerson Press, 1961.

Early Ontario Glass. Toronto: The Royal Ontario Museum, 1965.

Canadian Glass c. *1825-1925*. Toronto: The Ryerson Press, 1967.